327.7308
W63i

129041

DATE DUE			

WITHDRAWN
L. R. COLLEGE LIBRARY

WIT   AWN
L. R. C   E LIBRARY

IN SEARCH OF POLICY

IN SEARCH OF POLICY

THE UNITED STATES AND LATIN AMERICA

HOWARD J. WIARDA

CARL A. RUDISILL LIBRARY
LENOIR RHYNE COLLEGE

American Enterprise Institute for Public Policy Research
Washington and London

327.7308
W63i
129041
may 1984

Library of Congress Cataloging in Publication Data

Wiarda, Howard J., 1939–
   In search of policy.

   (AEI studies ; 396)
   1. Latin America—Foreign relations—United States—
Addresses, essays, lectures. 2. United States—Foreign
relations—Latin America—Addresses, essays, lectures.
I. Title.   II. Series.
F1418.W65   1984   327.7308   83–25670
ISBN 0–8447–3542–6
ISBN 0–8447–3541–8 (pbk.)

AEI Studies 396
1 3 5 7 9 10 8 6 4 2

©1984 by the American Enterprise Institute for Public Policy Research,
Washington, D.C., and London. All rights reserved. No part of this publication may be used or reproduced in any manner whatsoever without
permission in writing from the American Enterprise Institute except in the
case of brief quotations embodied in news articles, critical articles, or
reviews. The views expressed in the publications of the American Enterprise Institute are those of the authors and do not necessarily reflect the
views of the staff, advisory panels, officers, or trustees of AEI.

"American Enterprise Institute" and ⬭ are registered service marks of
the American Enterprise Institute for Public Policy Research.

Printed in the United States of America

To Kristy, Howard, Jonathan

The American Enterprise Institute for Public Policy Research, established in 1943, is a nonpartisan research and educational organization supported by foundations, corporations, and the public at large. Its purpose is to assist policy makers, scholars, businessmen, the press, and the public by providing objective analysis of national and international issues. Views expressed in the institute's publications are those of the authors and do not necessarily reflect the views of the staff, advisory panels, officers, or trustees of AEI.

Council of Academic Advisers

Paul W. McCracken, *Chairman, Edmund Ezra Day University Professor of Business Administration, University of Michigan*

*Kenneth W. Dam, *Harold J. and Marion F. Green Professor of Law, University of Chicago*

Donald C. Hellmann, *Professor of Political Science and International Studies, University of Washington*

D. Gale Johnson, *Eliakim Hastings Moore Distinguished Service Professor of Economics and Chairman, Department of Economics, University of Chicago*

Robert A. Nisbet, *Adjunct Scholar, American Enterprise Institute*

Herbert Stein, *A. Willis Robertson Professor of Economics, University of Virginia*

James Q. Wilson, *Henry Lee Shattuck Professor of Government, Harvard University*

*On leave for government service.

Executive Committee

Richard B. Madden, *Chairman of the Board*
William J. Baroody, Jr., *President*
James G. Affleck

Willard C. Butcher
Paul F. Oreffice
Richard D. Wood

Tait Trussell,
   Vice President, Administration
Joseph J. Brady,
   Vice President, Development

Edward Styles, *Director of Publications*

Program Directors

Russell Chapin, *Legislative Analyses*
Denis P. Doyle, *Education Policy Studies*
Marvin Esch, *Seminars and Programs*
Thomas F. Johnson, *Economic Policy Studies*
Marvin H. Kosters,
   Government Regulation Studies
Jack A. Meyer, *Health Policy Studies*
Howard R. Penniman/Austin Ranney,
   Political and Social Processes
Robert J. Pranger, *International Programs*

Periodicals

AEI Economist, Herbert Stein,
   Editor
Public Opinion, Seymour Martin
   Lipset and Ben J. Wattenberg,
   Co-Editors; Everett Carll Ladd,
   Senior Editor; Karlyn H. Keene,
   Managing Editor
Regulation, Anne Brunsdale,
   Managing Editor

Contents

Foreword

Latin America has become increasingly important to the United States, and it affects us in a large variety of ways. For one thing, our trade with Latin America has grown enormously in recent decades; for another, we have become preoccupied with the strategic situation in Central America; for a third, we have become concerned with the impact on our own society of large-scale and uncontrolled immigration from that area. The drug traffic, our need for petroleum and other resources, our concern for democracy and human rights, the debt situation, and other factors all force us to give serious attention to Latin America and U.S. policy toward the region.

In this book Howard J. Wiarda, director of the Center for Hemispheric Studies at the American Enterprise Institute, explores the nature of the U.S.–Latin American relationship. He presents the history of U.S.–Latin American relations, spells out the assumptions and biases that undergird the attitudes of the United States toward Latin America, and suggests why our policies so often go astray and how we might achieve a more effective and more enlightened policy. The book, strongly public policy oriented, contains major recommendations that deserve consideration.

Readers are likely to find Dr. Wiarda's analysis of the tendency to see the region only in terms of our own needs and goals that has dominated American foreign policy toward Latin America challenging and provocative. In the several chapters he explores the North-South dialogue, the aftermath of the Falklands/Malvinas controversy, revolution in Nicaragua, change and continuity in U.S. policy, the origins of the crisis in the Caribbean basin, U.S. policy in El Salvador and Central America, and the problem of conceptual failure in U.S. Latin American policy. In the final chapter he puts forth a positive approach—what he calls a "prudence model" of U.S.-Latin American relations.

This book is another in a series of books and research reports published by AEI on Latin America and U.S.-Latin American relations. AEI has become a major center of public policy research on

Latin America, and our Center for Hemispheric Studies has gained a national and international reputation for its work in this area. We have published extensively on U.S.–Latin American trade relations, security policy, foreign assistance, and a great many other subjects. We intend to remain in the forefront of the serious study of these issues.

Howard Wiarda is one of the nation's leading scholars on Latin America and a prolific writer. Particularly as American foreign policy has become increasingly engaged in this area, his comments on the biases, misplaced assumptions, and lack of understanding that often characterize U.S. policy toward Latin America take on added importance. He is not just a scholar writing in the abstract but one who has for a number of years been actively involved in the formulation of policy. For these and other reasons, his dissection of U.S. Latin American policy and his recommendations for new perspectives and change merit serious attention.

WILLIAM J. BAROODY, JR.
President, American Enterprise Institute
Washington, D.C.

Preface

The essays, papers, and statements of testimony collected here were all written in Washington, D.C., between 1981 and 1983 during the author's initial tenure as resident scholar and director of the Center for Hemispheric Studies at the American Enterprise Institute for Public Policy Research. They deal with the themes, ideas, attitudes, and theories prevailing in inter-American relations and are informed both by the greater sense of "insiderness" that living in Washington provides and by the special "window on the world" that comes from the AEI affiliation.

This collection focuses on the history, background, biases, assumptions, and prejudices that undergird U.S. Latin American policy. At the root of our problems with Latin America, this volume suggests, is a lack of understanding and comprehension of the area, a pervasive ethnocentrism, and a lack of empathy. The book is hence infused by both an ethical sense of what a better policy ought to be and a scholarly analysis of the bases of policy in the past. A planned follow-up monograph will deal more extensively with the processes of foreign policy making, how policy gets made, how it works or fails to work, based largely on what I have seen and heard in Washington from the particular perch that I occupy.

The papers presented here, in seeking to correct a major bias often present in the literature and in our policy analyses of Latin America, were written in considerable measure from the point of view of improving broader *hemispheric* understanding and *inter-American* relations, as contrasted with the usual perspective, which is U.S. policy *toward* Latin America. That is, instead of writing from a strictly U.S. perspective, I have tried to understand and balance both sides of the inter-American equation. The unfortunate facts are not only that we do not comprehend Latin America very well but that Latin Americans do not understand the United States very well either.

Through greater knowledge and understanding, these essays argue, U.S. interests and Latin American development may be pursued in tandem and compatibly. This perspective leads to policy prescriptions that imply greater caution, realism, restraint, pragmatism, empathy, understanding, and balance. These ingredients have often been absent from U.S.–Latin American relations in the past, but I am convinced that a policy based on these features serves in the longer run both our own interests and those of Latin America.

The papers included have been lightly edited from their original versions to ensure accuracy and timeliness. Pamela Robertson has typed and retyped these chapters, and to her I am grateful. Janine Perfit has done splendid work as a research assistant. Dr. Iêda Siqueira Wiarda has, as in the past, provided numerous editorial suggestions and ideas; her contributions are especially valuable because of the spirit, *en familia*, in which they are offered. But it is to the younger generation, now maturing and with ideas of their own—Kristy, Howard, Jonathan—that the book is dedicated, with the hope that the empathy and understanding that I see as so essential in inter-American relations prevails more in the new generation than in the older one.

1
Cancún and After: The United States and the Developing World

The meeting of heads of state and foreign ministers of the eight industrialized and the fourteen developing nations (why these nations were invited and not others remains something of a mystery to those not invited) held at Mexico's lush island resort of Cancún in October 1981 raised high hopes and expectations among some, consternation and frustration among others. The real meaning and substance of the meeting were often obscured by the media's forced reliance on the official press briefings and, in the absence of other information, the emphasis on the food eaten, the elaborate security precautions, and the luxury of the surroundings. By now Cancún has faded from the headlines, but the issues and agendas raised are likely to be with us for a long time.

The Cancún meeting may have been a watershed. It is not that the place is so important or even that this particular gathering was so crucial. The issues have been building for years. But what Cancún did was to provide a prestigious forum and sounding board for third-world ideas and to bring some of these home to the American public for the first time. Among other things Cancún served to illustrate how isolated the United States is internationally not just from the developing nations but often from its allies as well; how much we have become dependent on many third-world nations for raw materials, commodities, and markets; the degree to which future agendas of international agencies and conferences will be dominated by third-world demands that the United States lower its protective tariff walls (with all the potential for disruptions of the domestic economy that implies) and that ways be found for major transfers of wealth from North to South; and last but certainly not least, whether the United States may not have already, in effect, lost the cold war so far as the nations of the developing world are concerned.

This paper appeared in *PS*, vol. 15 (Winter 1982).

The Economic Agenda

Both Cancún and the unsatisfactorily incomplete North-South dialogue have pitted the "have" nations against the "have-nots." Within both these camps there exist further divisions. Many of the poorer or less developed countries (LDCs) would like to focus on the issue of a debt moratorium; others are presently seeking new financing and do not want to make the lenders nervous with such talk. The have-nots are also divided into oil-rich and oil-scarce nations; into those who are "making it" (the newly industrialized countries, or NICs, such as Brazil, Mexico, Venezuela, South Korea) and those, the vast majority, who are not (the correlations between these two sets of categories are not one-to-one: Venezuela is oil-rich, Brazil is not). The industrialized nations are often divided between the presently more conservatively governed Anglo-American nations (except perhaps Trudeau's Canada) and the socialist and social-democratic nations of the Continent, many of whom side in varying degrees with third-world aims. The divisions exist, and they make for dramatic headlines; but it is equally clear that the United States has become increasingly isolated in such forums.

While the third world is divided on some issues, it has remained remarkably unified for almost two decades now on the basic demand for a fundamental reallocation of the world's wealth. The agenda includes more and easier credit terms, better access to Northern markets for goods manufactured in the third world, higher and stabler prices for the primary goods the third world exports, and easier terms for the purchase of oil. These are clearly negotiable and not unreasonable goals, but they have often been obscured by the rhetoric of "massive transfers of wealth," which the major Northern countries find unacceptable.

The locus of such discussions is of course critical to their outcome, and here again trouble is brewing. The developing nations have pressed to hold discussions on the major issues above in the United Nations General Assembly, a forum in which they hold not only an enormous majority but which is perilously close to being dominated by the Communist nations, their clientela, and the more radical of the third-world bloc (such as Libya or Cuba).[1] The United States prefers to hold discussions in agencies or forums such as the World Bank, the General Agreement on Tariffs and Trade, or the International Monetary Fund, which it has in the past been able to dominate. But it should be emphasized that these agencies have also been under intense pressure in recent years to provide greater third-world representation and to accommodate its demands; the trend has clearly been in that direction.

The United States, while providing limited public assistance (the measurement of which is open to diverse interpretations), has recently urged a strategy of private initiative and free-enterprise capitalism as a means of development for the third world; and a new office has been created within the State Department's Agency for International Development to promote that strategy. Privately, some administration officials admit that will not work in societies where there is no or only a weak entrepreneurial class; and one suspects the administration's position is actually based on the following considerations: the president's own strongly held beliefs, the need to satisfy a significant U.S. political and economic constituency, and the interest of some U.S. major industries such as oil. But in a world in which in virtually every other country except the United States, and especially in the developing nations, greater statism rather than less seems to be both the preferred way and the almost inevitable result of increasing global economic complexity and interdependence, expanded, social pressures and services, and the perceived need for state guidance and control of turbulent economic pressures, such a policy is unlikely to prove realistic. Fortunately, Mr. Reagan seems to be a good listener; and if the right voices get to him, he can be persuaded that conditions in Santo Domingo or Sri Lanka are different from those in Iowa or Illinois. For example, the administration's Caribbean Basin Initiative represents a blend of public and private involvement not much different from Kennedy's Alliance for Progress.

While U.S. advocacy of laissez-faire capitalism is not likely to find great receptivity in the third world, and while the administration has often been more pragmatic than its own rhetoric might lead one to infer, the third world's own prescription of immediate and massive transfers of wealth from North to South has often been equally unrealistic. In the long run, however, one suspects that a good part of its program is likely to be realized. The third world feels that time, morality, and worldwide public opinion will eventually work in its favor. And if one recognizes the degree of vulnerability and dependence that the United States and the rest of the industrialized world have or soon will have on third-world resources (the United States sells more goods to developing countries than to Japan and Western Europe combined; markets in the third world are growing faster than those of any other area), the strength and solidarity of new OPEC-like cartels (the demand for bananas is, admittedly, less inelastic than that for oil, but wait until we see what happens to the price of such essentials as copper, manganese, or bauxite), and the trends in the international forums where many of these issues will be decided (increasingly away from the United States), the prospects seem to favor the third world. Each American administration of course hopes it will be out of office when the real crunch comes, but there is a lurking suspicion that in the massive foreign debt situation, the third world may have already found the mechanism for the massive transfer of wealth it has been seeking.

Cancún provided an opening for changes in the relations between the first and third world and, with Mr. Reagan present, a legitimacy heretofore lacking for the third world's demands. The United States may choose not to go any further than it already has in responding to the third-world agenda; but if it selects that option, it will not only be further isolated but also will run the risk, now that the impetus to alter the international system has begun, that it may eventually find itself with no other choice than to go along. The situation is roughly analogous to that governing the Law of the Sea Treaty negotiations. The United States does not like various provisions in the proposed treaty and may well choose to continue acting unilaterally with regard to certain sea and seabed activities; but if the treaty is then implemented anyway by the rest of the world, the United States may be forced to accept in one form or another its major precepts. That is in any case the strategy the third world has adopted with regard to the LOS treaty, and it is undoubtedly what the third world will do with regard to the transfer-of-wealth issue should the United States stand entirely against any further negotiations.

At Cancún Mr. Reagan was cordial but noncommittal, and the U.S. statement was crafted carefully to be purposely ambiguous, to make it appear that the United States would not stonewall all future discussions, to say no (or perhaps maybe) in a cooperative way. The statement emphasized that third-world nations should first improve their domestic economic policies, which could be translated as meaning they should expect no increases in U.S. aid, and that future talks should take place in a forum where there is a "cooperative spirit," which means not the General Assembly. The statement meant to give the impression of progress while also implying a U.S. holding action.

In the meantime there remains room for bargaining over more concrete, less grandiose issues. That is undoubtedly a further aspect of the U.S. strategy. These include such issues as bilateral foreign assistance and loans in their many forms, the lowering of U.S. tariff walls on select third-world products, some easing of credit restrictions, and assistance to help finance discovery and production of oil and other fuels in the third world. Negotiations over these narrower issues will be protracted, enabling the United States to adjust and compromise and play for time; but the other and larger issues will remain.

The Political Agenda

From the beginning the Cancún conference involved politics at least as much as economics. The decision to exclude Cuba's Fidel Castro from the proceedings, the condition under which President Reagan agreed to attend, and the decision of Mr. Reagan himself to go to Cancún, given the potential pitfalls and the avoidance by American presidents of such forums in the past, served as preludes to the actual discussions at the conference itself and were all preeminently political matters. The issues *at* Cancún were also political, involving the willingness of the Northern nations to negotiate, where such negotiations should take place, and the power such chosen bodies should have. Cancún did not involve discussions over the appropriate price for tomatoes or cucumbers.

The differences within and between the blocs represented are also primarily political. Both blocs are misnamed, though the issues dividing them are fairly clear-cut. The less industrialized nations, referred to as the "South" but whose ranks include India, Yugoslavia, and others north of the equator, saw Cancún as a means to reinvigorate the global negotiations that have been largely stalled for the past three years. And it is mainly for political reasons that the South hopes to vest ultimate decision making on such negotiations in a body, the General Assembly, where voting is in terms of one-nation, one-vote, thus guaranteeing the South will prevail at least at the formal ballot level. The fact must also be faced realistically that conducting further negotiations in the UN agencies is certain to involve political efforts by the Soviet Union and its clients in the third world at further isolating the United States internationally, using the discussions as a propaganda forum, and embarrassing the United States by trying to wrench unacceptable concessions from it.

The "North" is no less a misnomer. Conspicuous by its absence is the Soviet Union, a northern and a comparatively developed nation, which refused to attend the Cancún meeting and spurns all such North-South dialogues on the grounds that only the "colonialist" and "imperialist" Western countries bear responsibility for the world's poverty. Should the discussions move to the UN, however, the Soviet Union and its now numerous bloc would surely side with the South. Nor, as indicated, are the Western allies themselves united: Britain under Mrs. Thatcher has generally supported the United States, while

5

France and Germany have increasingly followed more independent policies, and the Netherlands, Sweden, and others are inclined to side with the third world.

The Northern nations, primarily the United States as we have seen, had heretofore resisted any global bargaining in a forum where small nations like Grenada would have a voice equal to that of the largest and richest countries. The United States had preferred those agencies (GATT, World Bank, IMF) where voting is weighted toward those who make the largest financial contribution or have the largest global interests.

It is generally agreed that in the international economic order there are four main means, in descending order of importance, by which the Northern nations have maintained their preeminence: (1) the structure of the world market economy through which the industrial nations dominate most major markets; (2) the framework of rules designed to maintain order and stability in world markets; (3) the national rules that are geared to promote and protect domestic markets, industry, and trade and that affect the third world not least by the sheer size of the rich economies in comparison with the weaker ones; and (4) buying and selling at the operational level where the largest countries and their firms have numerous advantages.[2] If this categorization is valid, then institutions like the GATT and the IMF can be considered a part of category 2, in which, by design and by definition, the economically strong are favored.

The idea that one might or ought to reform the international economic order is not new. In the contemporary setting Nkrumah, Tito, Nyere, Castro, and, most recently, Willy Brandt have been important spokesmen. Raúl Prebisch and the Economic Commission for Latin America (ECLA) had earlier provided much of the intellectual justification by emphasizing the widening gaps in the present international economic system between those countries that are chiefly exporters of primary goods and those that export manufactured products. Rather than narrowing, the gap between the developed and the developing (or expecting-to-develop) nations was bound to widen; hence the demand for a redress of such imbalances. It is important to emphasize the degree of unanimity among the Southern nations on the fundamental flaws in the existing international system and the reasons for them.

The Southern nations, moreover, were skillful in presenting their case.[3] The UN resolution calling for the establishment of a "new international economic order" and for the "elimination" of the "widening gap between the developed and the developing countries" was passed at the Sixth Session of the General Assembly in April 1974. The timing was not accidental. It came on the heels of the malfunctioning of the Bretton Woods system, the first round of major hikes in oil prices, an unsettled period in commodity prices, and at the onset of a world-wide economic slump. These events revealed both the vulnerability of the industrialized countries as never before and the divisions among them as they all scrambled individually to secure their oil supplies. Not only was the economic insecurity of the North thus made obvious, but the international political framework of its dominance also seemed wobbly. In presenting their demands the Southern nations undoubtedly overemphasized the Northerners' vulnerability and the opportunity for advantage it afforded. Nonetheless the Southerners did see a chance to press ahead on the redistributional agenda that they had long advocated but lacked the strength and opportunity to implement. They gained some success via the Brandt Commission report and in other forums, but it was precisely the stalling and frustration of their further efforts that led to the call for the Cancún meeting.

Essentially what Cancún was all about was the Southerners' efforts to present their case to a president who was initially opposed but whom they hoped would be open-minded and to attempt to persuade Mr. Reagan to moderate however slightly the U.S. opposition to global negotiations within a forum such as the UN. In this overarching task they feel they achieved success, though the language of the communiqués emanating from Cancún remained vague and future steps are still undecided. The United States will doubtless go along with the idea of some limited "global" negotiations, but the degree to which these will be diluted is still not certain. One low-ranking U.S. official has said of such negotiations that "we support them as long as they don't get results."

More constructively, others are exploring whether it is possible that a UN agency might review but not veto decisions taken at the GATT or the IMF, or whether small negotiating groups representing member states' interests and composed mainly of experts from the nations affected and not members of the UN missions might be established for discussing particular issues. In the absence of agreement by the key parties no obligations would be involved. Conditions might also be imposed, by others as well as by the United States, on the outcome of such negotiations or the nature of the negotiations themselves.[4] The General Assembly might still vote on these matters, but its actions would be, as on other issues, more hortatory than substantive. Having committed itself to negotiations, however, the United States would likely find it very difficult to resist any concessions whatsoever. In this sense Cancún and Mr. Reagan's presence there were a major victory and opening wedge for the third world's redistributional program.

The Social Science Agenda

The methodologies and prevailing developmental approaches of the social sciences were not on the formal agenda at Cancún; nor at a meeting of heads of state would one expect them to be. Nevertheless such concerns loom undeniably in the background among the intellectual elites that help advise heads of state in the third world and among some of the state leaders themselves. Certainly such concerns are prominent as underlying influences in the international forums in which the economic and political agendas mentioned above are and will be discussed. The matter should be of particular interest to policy makers.

The issue is this: Not only have many third-world leaders and intellectuals rejected the presumption of economic and political hegemony long held by the Northern nations, but they have also come to reject many of the social science notions underlying such assumptions and that condemn them to a status of inferiority and "underdevelopment." The emerging nations no longer believe or accept that they are but pale and retarded imitations of the West fated to follow its same developmental stages, that the West offers both lessons and a model from which they can learn or which they must imitate, or that the Western experience of a small group of countries in the north of Europe and America in the nineteenth century provides *the* developmental formula that they both ought to imitate in an ethical sense and *must* follow in accord with the unfolding of an inevitable historical process.[5]

Third-world leaders tend to see the developmental literature of the 1960s, which once enjoyed so much popularity as the dominant interpretive paradigm, as biased, ethnocentric, and prejudicial, insensitive to their own distinct histories and cultures and often running roughshod over them, inimical to and sometimes mocking of their often revered traditional institutions, helping to perpetuate myths about third-world backwardness and Western superiority not just in an economic sense but politically, socially, and often morally as well, hostile and damaging to indigenous ways and institutions, and wrought with, to them, irrelevant cold war overtones. As the United States primarily and Western Europe secondarily have lost both will and strength to serve as policemen of the world, and as their economies have proved vulnerable, the social science concepts that often undergirded the Western sense of dominance and superiority have come increasingly under attack as well.

Along with the attack on the presumed superiority and universality of the social science models derived from the West have come a new concern and search for indigenous concepts of development. In part these lie behind the resurgence of Islamic fundamentalism and the notion of an Islamic state, law, and society; behind the reexamination by third-world leaders of such institutions as India's caste associations and African tribalism, which Western developmental political sociology had largely confined to the dustbins of "tradition" and discarded history but which numerous third-world leaders are now reconsidering as possible bases for new and indigenous societal forms; and behind the resurgence of corporate and organic-statist models (in a variety of types) throughout Latin America. Within the third world, hence, and as a reflection of these trends, efforts are being made to formulate an Islamic social science of development, an Indian social science of development, a sub-Saharan African social science of development, a Latin American social science of development, and so on.[6]

Some perspective is necessary. The comments above are not meant to minimize the wrenching conflicts within the third world over such issues, the divisions and sheer confusion à la Naipaul that exist, the pull that the West still has. The dilemma for many third-world leaders is thus not whether to turn their backs on the West but how to modernize without necessarily Westernizing, how to use the capital and technology of the West without accepting the social and political concomitants that often accompany such changes, how to achieve, in novelist Carlos Fuentes's words, the health, wealth, and efficiency of the West without sacrificing deep ethical and cultural roots or the viability of historical and often preferred institutions. This is a fundamental dilemma that corresponds with another: how to reconcile the rising expectations of third-world peoples as well as their growing consciousness of their own identity and interests *with* the traditional power and high living standards of the industrialized North. This growing awareness of cultural and political diversity in the third world and the need for a different balance between their own and imported institutions, between what is distinctive and what is universal in each nation's or culture area's development process, is related to the growing assertiveness of the third world and its demands in the economic and political spheres, at Cancún and elsewhere.

Conclusion

Cancún provided new-found momentum for third-world concerns while also interjecting some realism into the debate. There will be no wholesale or immediate transfer of wealth from North to South, but there is abundant room for compromise over such issues as lower tariff barriers for third-world products; the debt; a greater third-world voice at the GATT, the IMF, and the World Bank; bilateral tax and investment treaties; energy; multilateral coverage to encourage investment; etc. Compromise is also possible on the respective forums for such discussions, involving studies, hearings, and exhortations at the UN combined with hard bargaining in agencies like the World Bank. It is also possible that the hortatory advocacy of massive transfers of wealth may in part be replaced by mutually beneficial collaboration that seeks to create new wealth and jobs in *both* the North and the South.

At Cancún the United States demonstrated its willingness to listen, bend somewhat, and perhaps compromise; and at present renewed discussions are under way in the U.S. government for the appropriate forums (perhaps not the General Assembly but a modified Cancún of "select" countries) and mechanisms to deal with the ensuing discussions. That is a hopeful sign, but there are major limiting factors as well. The domestic mood would not appear propitious for either much greater foreign assistance or the lowering of tariff barriers that cost U.S. jobs; nor would Congress or the White House be likely to initiate such steps, certainly not in an election year. The United States has said that it will listen to third-world grievances, but the context of increasing U.S. isolation internationally, mounting pressures for protectionism, waning patience with both the third world's demands and the UN agencies from which they ensue, coupled with shaky and in some cases near-bankrupted economies in the third world and mounting social, economic, and political pressures both at home and abroad, must be kept in mind. And even if the United States does listen, the gaps of empathy and understanding are so great as to lead in all likelihood to greater disjunction and conflict rather than to any mutual understanding. As a rich, powerful, and comparatively conservative nation, the United States may be willing to provide some economic and technical aid; but a true understanding of third-world cultures, problems, aspirations, and special needs— and from the third world's own point of view—seems remote. Political and social scientists could help bridge these gaps, but as indicated, the models of development they have espoused in the past are often part and parcel of the same ethnocentric assumptions underlying our assistance program.

The third world's requests have a powerful logic and legitimacy behind them from the point of view of both international social justice and the requirements of contemporary economic interdependence between North and South. In our present circumstances of economic recession, political isolation, and growing dependence on third-world resources, we may come to recognize that we may need the third-world almost as much as it needs us. Hence the discussions that follow Cancún will depend on both the different national and bloc interests represented *and* the attitudes that all parties assume. Cancún may be seen as one of the initial steppingstones in what will surely be a long passage. But the journey will certainly not be made easier, even if the will and favorable U.S. political circumstances are present, by the conditions of global economic downturns, recession, and stagnant or contracting economies in which both the North and the South now find themselves.

Notes

1. An amusing but also discouraging account of one such, not unrepresentative UN forum is Walter Berns, "Where the Majority Rules: A UN Diary," *The American Spectator,* vol. 14 (November 1981), pp. 7–12.

2. Susan Strange, *Sterling and British Policy* (London: Oxford University Press, 1971); and Peter C. J. Vale, "North-South Relations and the Lomé Conventions: Treating the Symptoms and Not the Causes" (Braamfontein: South African Institute of International Affairs, July 1981).

3. The analysis follows that of Vale, "North-South Relations."

4. Some reasonable suggestions for such negotiations have been set forth in an Op-Ed statement by former Ambassador Richard N. Gardner, "Beyond Cancún," *New York Times,* November 8, 1981.

5. These ideas have been elaborated and analyzed in considerably greater detail by the author in two papers: Howard J. Wiarda, "The Ethnocentrism of the Social Sciences: Implications for Research and Policy," *The Review of Politics,* vol. 43 (April 1981), pp. 163–97; and "Toward a Non-Ethnocentric Theory of Development: Alternative Conceptions from the Third World," *Journal of Developing Areas* (Fall 1983).

6. See, on this theme, Edward Said, *Orientalism* (New York: Pantheon, 1978); G. H. Jansen, *Militant Islam* (New York: Harper & Row, 1980); Vrajenda Raj Mehta, *Beyond Marxism: Toward an Alternative Perspective* (New Delhi: Manohar Publications, 1978); Howard J. Wiarda, *Corporatism and National Development in Latin America* (Boulder, Colo.: Westview Press, 1981); Howard J. Wiarda, ed., *Politics and Social Change in Latin America: The Distinct Tradition,* 2d rev. ed. (Amherst: University of Massachusetts Press, 1982). Additional literature and sources on these themes are cited in the two articles in note 5.

2

The United States and Latin America in the Aftermath of the Falklands/Malvinas Crisis

Introduction

In the media and public discussion of U.S.–Latin American relations in the aftermath of the Falklands/Malvinas controversy of 1982, two interpretations have been dominant. One suggests that U.S.–Latin American relations have been newly, severely, and perhaps irrevocably damaged by the U.S. posture of siding with the British in the conflict. The other suggests that relatively little damage has been done and that after a decent interval U.S.–Latin American relations will stabilize and return to normal.

I wish to suggest a third and, I think, more accurate position, which also borrows from the other two. I believe, on the one hand, that U.S.–Latin American relations have been severely damaged by the U.S. posture and actions in this crisis. On the other hand, the Falklands/Malvinas controversy was only one, particularly dramatic event in a considerably longer history of declining and probably worsening U.S.–Latin American relations, viewed as an overall picture. Our bilateral relations with quite a number of individual countries are fairly good, but our relations with the area as a whole have been deteriorating.

The Falklands/Malvinas controversy will thus help accelerate tendencies long under way. A new plateau will doubtlessly be reached in U.S.–Latin American relations in the aftermath of the most recent controversy, but it will be at a lower, less amicable, less accommoda-

Presented before the Subcommittee on Inter-American Affairs, Committee on Foreign Affairs, United States House of Representatives, July 20, 1982; published in *Latin America and the United States after the Falklands/Malvinas Crisis: Hearings before the Subcommittee on Inter-American Affairs, Committee on Foreign Affairs, House of Representatives* (Washington, D.C.: GPO, 1982).

tive, possibly more conflictive level than in the past. In this sense it is perhaps accurate to say that our relations will eventually "stabilize" and return to "normal." But "normalcy" will have been restored in an overall context of tension, difficulty, and new conditions that augur even greater problems in the future.

The Essential Problems

The Congress is at least as cognizant of the basic attitudinal and policy problems plaguing U.S.–Latin American relations as are those who study the area. Let me summarize these briefly as a series of propositions, reserving further discussion and qualification if necessary for later.[1]

1. The United States is not very much interested in Latin America. That attitude is highlighted nicely in *New York Times* columnist James Reston's comment that "the United States will do anything for Latin America except read about it."

2. The United States does not believe Latin America is important. My own view is that immigration, economic interdependence, political priorities, proximity, and other factors are forcing us to change that assessment; but change will require some time and will be a long-term process.

3. U.S. policy is still primarily European-oriented. Moreover, as a country we tend to be Euro-centric. In this context, Latin America does not count for much. The Latin American countries are seen as second-class allies.

4. U.S. policy is crisis oriented, as in the recent Falklands/Malvinas controversy or as regards our attention to El Salvador in the past three years. The rest of the time we ignore the area.

5. Not only do we not read about Latin America or well understand its political culture, but we do not *wish* to understand it. Our images and comprehension of the area are often derived from old movies, simplistic formulas, and misleading popular stereotypes. These attitudes in turn are conditioned by long-time political, religious, racial, and cultural prejudices. In the recent Falklands/Malvinas controversy the racial, ethnic, and cultural slurs sometimes used—such as "tin-horn dictators" and "pock-marked generals"—were often little short of outrageous. We combine ignorance of the area with prejudice and not a little hostility.

6. When we *are* forced to turn our attention to Latin America, we tend to view it exclusively through U.S. lenses. *Our* criteria of separation of powers, human rights, civil-military relations, development,

and labor relations are the ones that are used. We seldom pay attention to what Latin America means or understands by such terms, and we are often unsympathetic to the notion that their practice not only differs from our own but also may be quite viable in Latin America's own context.[2]

7. We often use Latin America as a kind of living laboratory for experiments in U.S.-conceived social and political engineering—for example, agrarian reform, family planning, community development—or alternatively as a theater for the acting out of U.S. domestic political considerations. Examples of the latter include both the administration's efforts early on to portray the crisis in Central America as an East-West struggle in accord with its campaign rhetoric *and* the activities of its foes in using Central America to demonstrate their social-reformist credentials, even though such a posture may have little to do with the realities of the area. As my AEI colleague, syndicated columnist Nick Thimmesch has written, "Democrats usually rush to Latin America with civics books, sermons, hot broth, and contraceptive devices." Republicans, in contrast, usually ignore that huge landmass with its 350 million people and turn their attention to it chiefly when cold war concerns force it onto the front pages.

Implications for U.S.–Latin American Relations of the Falklands/Malvinas Controversy

Given the basic problems of ignorance, prejudice, and lack of empathy or understanding with regard to Latin America, which I would argue are at the heart of our difficult political and diplomatic relations with the area, let me turn now to the implications of the Falklands/Malvinas controversy for those relations. Again, these will be listed briefly and in proposition form, with the understanding that further elaboration and qualification are necessary.

The implications of the Falklands/Malvinas controversy for U.S.–Latin American relations seem to me severe, damaging, and long term. I do not see any good coming out of this crisis, nor do I see the damage being repaired easily or soon. At the same time it should be reiterated that this crisis is but one of many in a considerable history dating back some seventeen years and helping produce a major, long-term diminution in the presence, power, and influence of the United States throughout the hemisphere.

1. Our long-time "special relationship" with Latin America has been damaged severely and may be moribund. In this crisis, where the United States opted to choose its preferred ally, it chose Great

Britain. That choice was widely seen throughout the hemisphere as a choice between Latin American and Anglo-Saxon civilizations. One understands the reasons behind the choice and also the lack of love many Latin Americans and others have for the Argentines. Still, the choice was a stark one; and while informed Latin Americans understand the Realpolitik of the issue, they will not soon forget the choice made.

2. Anti-Americanism is now rampant. This is now true not only in those nations that have allied themselves with the Soviet Union but with friends such as Venezuela and Brazil as well. It is widespread not only among youth, organized labor, and the left, but in conservative and centrist circles as well. We are used to and expect anti-Americanism to come from the left; what bears emphasis in the present circumstances is the growth of rightist and centrist nationalism and anti-Americanism as well.

3. The North-South dispute has been intensified. Already heating up because of past grievances and perceived U.S. inaction, the Falklands/Malvinas controversy has been widely portrayed in Latin America and elsewhere as a deplorable case of aggression by the industrialized nations of the North against the third-world countries of the South. I cannot comment on the accuracy of these perceptions, but they are widely believed in Latin America, and there as here perceptions are often at least as important in politics as reality.

4. These sentiments all seem to me symptomatic of the long-term decline of U.S. influence in Latin America, of Latin American efforts to modify its position of dependency vis-à-vis the United States, of the diminishing presence of the United States in the area and our presumption of hemispheric hegemony, and of our declining control over Latin American affairs. Such attitudes did not originate in the Falklands/Malvinas crisis, but they have become more widespread as a result of it. As former Peace Corps director Joseph Blatchford has said, this crisis has accelerated the drift of the Latin American nations toward Western Europe, Japan, third worldism, perhaps even nonalignment and the Soviet Union because "that's the way the world is going these days."

5. The crisis also damaged U.S. credibility. Not only did we opt to side with the British, but even when we were ostensibly still neutral and involved in the negotiations as a peacemaker, we were actually aiding the British with intelligence information and in other ways. That fact has been more widely publicized in Latin America than in the United States.

6. The inter-American system has been severely damaged. The Rio Treaty, which we long nurtured as a bulwark against Communist

expansion, is all but defunct; the Organization of American States has become an anti-American forum; the whole range of inter-American agencies built up over decades is threatened; the dream of an inter-American peace force is unlikely now to be resuscitated; the old American hope of someday linking the North Atlantic Treaty Organization with the hemispheric alliance is now also gone.

7. My estimation is that there is almost certain to be an escalation of the arms race in Latin America. Not only will Argentina wish to rearm, but that will also set off a chain reaction in Brazil, Chile, Peru, Ecuador, Colombia, Venezuela, and Bolivia. The arms race may not be confined to conventional weapons; Argentina and then Brazil may move to develop a nuclear capacity, and Latin America will no longer be a nuclear-free zone.

8. In Argentina the internal results of this controversy have been enormous. An already deeply divided nation has fragmented still further, producing greater economic and political instability. Argentina cannot be seen any longer as serving as a U.S. accomplice in Central America. The better relations that had been developing between the United States and Argentina over the previous year and a half are gone. Argentina may reestablish "normal" relations with the United States, but "normalcy" in that relationship implies lingering deep distrust and considerable anti-Americanism.

9. The hand of the Soviet Union has been strengthened. The Soviets may well be the only nation to have gained from this crisis. This is not to imply a sudden movement of Latin America toward realignment with the Soviet Union; the Soviets will be kept at arm's length. But it does imply stronger trade, diplomatic, and commercial ties with the Soviets; new thrusts toward nonalignment and neutrality; and a lessening of the ties of dependence on the United States. In the longer term the crisis may also result in a stronger Soviet presence in such strategic areas as the South Atlantic or Antarctica.

10. The Falklands/Malvinas crisis has provided an additional anti-American club for the left in Latin America, while also enabling Cuba and Nicaragua, who sided publicly and loudly with Argentina, to break out of the hemispheric isolation to which they had increasingly been subjected.

11. U.S. relations with Latin America, public and private, have been made more difficult on a wide range of issues. Normal contacts are now somewhat more testy, diplomatic relations are strained, a host of cultural and exchange programs have been canceled. Latin America is not in a position to break with the United States or to impose overt sanctions against it, but there will be quiet sanctions. Consider this scenario told to me recently by a former Argentine

cabinet minister: that when there are contracts for dams, highways, and other projects, and when there are European, Japanese, and American bidders, we may be certain the U.S. firm will not get the contracts.

What Should the United States Do?

We argued earlier that the problems in U.S.-Latin American relations growing out of the Falklands/Malvinas crisis were mainly long term and, for that reason, difficult of resolution. That is, the crisis helped accelerate a process of estrangement that had been under way for some time, but the crisis itself was only the most recent in a long series of events that have had the cumulative impact of drawing the United States and Latin America farther and farther apart.

Because these differences are so basic and have been in the making for a long time, it is difficult to believe they can easily or quickly be resolved. Nevertheless some modest suggestions might be offered for improving relations somewhat—but without our becoming excessively optimistic (1) that these suggestions can easily be followed through, or (2) that at this stage they will lead to much improvement.

1. The United States should take steps to restore its special relationship with Latin America—or what is left of it. There *are* ties of history, culture, politics, peoples, religion, and a common New World heritage that deserve emphasis. We may wish, for example, to reemphasize our common quest for democratic government, but in the present context we cannot seek to impose our institutional preferences on Latin America. Rather, we must empathize with Latin America's own institutional development and its efforts to fashion viable institutions in accord with its own history and culture.

2. We must begin to restore the inter-American system. That may mean a revamped OAS, a revamped security treaty arrangement, etc. Whether and to what degree that is still feasible remains to be seen.

3. We need to move forward quickly with the Caribbean Basin Initiative. Whether that is possible in an election year and with the array of forces lined up against it, the members of the Subcommittee [on Inter-American Affairs] can judge better than I. If we do not accept the CBI, however, presently democratic countries like the Dominican Republic or Costa Rica, faced with immense economic difficulties, may very soon become new El Salvadors.

4. In all these areas we must remember that action is required, not rhetoric. There has been much talk about why we did what we did in the Falklands/Malvinas controversy; now what Latin America is look-

ing for are concrete steps preferably in the economic sphere. Actions on trade, tariff, and market issues will speak far louder than words.

5. We must stop meddling in the internal affairs of countries whose traditions and politics are often different from our own and which we only weakly comprehend. I am opposed to either U.S. ambassadors or congressmen exercising essentially proconsular roles in countries to which they are assigned or visit and to their seeking to impose their preferred solutions on countries where these may be inappropriate.[3] We all understand that the granting of U.S. assistance carries with it an obligation on the part of the United States to see that the funds are appropriately spent, but there are ways to do this with sensitivity and without the heavy-handedness that we have frequently seen recently. Such interventions in Latin American internal affairs only breed greater resentments and anti-Americanism.

6. On a longer-term basis, we must strengthen our cultural exchanges and our languages and area studies programs. The fact is that we do not understand Latin America very well and Latin America does not understand the United States. These misconceptions and misreadings on both sides were particularly evident in the Falklands/Malvinas controversy.

7. We should begin discussions and hearings on the relative importance to be assigned the diverse world regions with which we must deal. Is our Euro-centrism still justified, or must other areas be elevated in importance? I have seen figures recently that the United States now has more trade with the third world than with Western Europe and Japan combined. I think a fundamental reassessment, based on such hard economic and political-strategic data, is now due on the relative importance of the world's areas with which we have important relations.

8. We must show greater restraint in using Latin America either as a laboratory for social and political experimentation or as a backdrop for political pronouncements and posturing designed chiefly for domestic political purposes. The pressure to command a headline is large, and Latin America is not usually in a position to retaliate; but the fact is we do and say things with regard to Latin America we would not dream of doing with regard to Europe, the Soviet Union, China, or the Middle East. The stakes by now are too high for us to continue taking our Latin American alliances for granted.

9. The Falklands/Malvinas controversy illustrated again the need for good intelligence, clear signals, firmness, and unambiguous directions in foreign policy. To one degree or another, all of these were faulty or lacking in the South Atlantic crisis. Some foreign policy "looseness" is perhaps inevitable in the kind of pluralist and demo-

cratic society we are, but there is also much room for greater coherence and coordination of policy.

10. We need to be more cognizant of and discriminating with regard to the dynamics of Latin American politics. Our discussion in this and other crises is often couched in terms of a presumed struggle between dictatorship and democracy. I submit this is a wrong and dangerous dichotomy when applied to Latin America that rules out various mixed solutions. It forces Latin America into a rigid political straitjacket and into a situation of choice divorced from its own political realities; it rules out the possibilities for various halfway houses between these polar points; and it in fact denies what has long been the genius of Latin American politics and politicians in devising fused, improvised, and ad hoc solutions. Yet it is precisely these mixed and ad hoc arrangements that enable Latin America to adjust to crises, accommodate to change, and go forward with development efforts.

11. Above all, I would call for a new era of tolerance, empathy, and understanding with regard to Latin America. For too long our attitudes toward the area have been characterized by ignorance, disdain, condescension, and a certain vague hostility. These were all strongly reflected in the Falklands/Malvinas controversy. It is time that we put these prejudices aside and began to understand Latin America not on strictly U.S. terms but in its own context, language, and setting. Latin America will and must fashion its own developmental model, independent of U.S. preferences. It is time that we let Latin America be Latin America.

I have been urging such restraint, empathy, and understanding toward Latin America for some twenty years. That experience, one may well understand, does not lead one to be overly optimistic as to the possibilities for easily or quickly altering very many basic attitudes and foreign policy premises with regard to that area. My students and much of the younger generation understand the necessity of reordering our priorities as suggested here, and for some unaccustomed modesty and deference in our attitudes, pronouncements, and policy toward Latin America. But among more senior officials and in policy-making quarters, among both Republicans and Democrats, the interventionist urge, the presumption that we know best for Latin America, remains powerful. That presumption, and the often naive, ill-informed, and ethnocentric policy initiatives that flow from it, lie at the root of our problems with Latin America.

Hearings such as these can provide a useful forum for bringing that message to policy makers and opinion leaders and for continuing discussion of the appropriate and proper role of the United States in Latin America. That role, it seems to me, in the changed circumstances of the present, requires that we avoid the sense of superiority tinged with dislike with which we have always looked at Latin America, and that we begin to exercise understanding, empathy, and comprehension of Latin America's efforts to develop autonomously, on its own, and in terms of its own institutional arrangements. At the least the Falklands/Malvinas crisis should alert us to the intense nationalistic feelings throughout the area and the desire to "go it alone" if necessary, and to the fact that Latin America can no longer be counted upon automatically to ally itself with the United States.

Notes

1. These arguments have been presented at greater length in my books, *Politics and Social Change in Latin America: The Distinct Tradition*, 2d. rev. ed. (Amherst: University of Massachusetts Press, 1982); *The Continuing Struggle for Democracy in Latin America* (Boulder, Colo.: Westview Press, 1980); and *Corporatism and National Development in Latin America* (Boulder, Colo.: Westview Press, 1981). See also the arguments set forth in a special issue of the *AEI Foreign Policy and Defense Review*, vol. 4, no. 2 (1982), devoted to "The Crisis in Central America."

2. These arguments are elaborated in a provocative fashion in my essay "Is Latin America Democratic—And Does It Want to Be?" in *The Continuing Struggle for Democracy in Latin America*.

3. As applied to the human rights issue and the different understandings between the United States and Latin America, see my essay entitled "Democracy and Human Rights in Latin America: Toward a New Conceptualization," *Orbis* (Spring 1978); reprinted in *Human Rights and U.S. Human Rights Policy* (Washington, D.C.: American Enterprise Institute, 1982).

3

The United States and Latin America: Change and Continuity

The Context of U.S. Latin American Policy

Latin America and Latin American policy in the United States are often discussed in impassioned, partisan, and intensely ideological terms that have little to do with either the Latin American area itself or actual U.S. policy toward that region. The issue of the moment may be Cuba, Nicaragua, El Salvador, human rights, the Malvinas/Falklands controversy, or some other hot issue or trouble spot. But the fact is in all these matters we tend to use Latin America to act out our own private or political dramas, as a locus for social experimentation we would be hesitant to attempt in the United States itself, as a sounding board and foil for our ideological likes and dislikes, or as a reflection of political considerations that are as often domestic as international.[1]

As a contiguous and presumably "Western" area, Latin America receives more of our attention than do most other third-world regions. Yet since it is weak and "underdeveloped," we know it cannot retaliate for the sins of omission and commission—to say nothing of the benefits—that we regularly shower upon it. Latin America therefore has, if not a "special relationship" with the United States, then certainly a "special place" in our political discourse, as a kind of *tabula rasa* for new foreign policy postures and initiatives that we would be far less anxious to try out on other world stages. All this is not meant to disparage the high motives, best intentions, and good deeds of many of those Americans who turn their attention to Latin America; but it is to say that Latin America has historically occupied a peculiar, frequently emotional or at least emotive position in our thinking and

Presented at the University of Pittsburgh Conference on the Caribbean, October 28–29, 1982, published in Alan Edelman and Reid Reading, eds., *Stability/Instability in the Caribbean Basin* (Pittsburgh: University of Pittsburgh Press, forthcoming).

policy, not all of which can be explained by the usual terms of reference of international politics. The subject merits greater attention than we can give it here.[2]

These comments are offered not just in passing but as a way of beginning to talk about the broad context of U.S.–Latin American relations. Let us state some unpleasant but necessary truths. The first is that Latin America has not historically been considered very significant in terms of a global U.S. foreign policy. Other areas—Western Europe, the Soviet Union, Asia, the Middle East—are thought of as more strategic or deserving of a higher priority. We do not often send our best personnel, private or public, to Latin America; and to a considerable extent even today a Latin American assignment, let alone specialization, is not always considered beneficial to one's career. Strategically, politically, economically, and culturally, the sad fact is that Latin America is seldom thought of as meriting serious, prolonged, or high-level attention.

The second unpleasant truth is that the United States does not have much sympathetic rapport with Latin America or its culture. We consistently view it through the prism of our own preferred solutions rather than in its own terms or context, to say nothing of language.[3] We seldom study the area and prefer to ignore it—until some new crisis forces it onto our television screens if not our consciences. We consistently apply U.S. solutions to solve its problems—whether these are applicable in Latin America or not. Equally consistently, we insist on interpreting Latin America in the political terms and ideological presuppositions appropriate for the United States or Western Europe, but generally with only limited relevance to Latin America. We seldom take the time to acquire more than a superficial acquaintance with Latin American history, culture, institutions, social structures and processes, or the dynamics of its political systems.

This leads, hence, to a third unpleasant truth about Latin America: not only do we not empathize with the area and its culture very well, but also we often prefer our biases and prejudices to any deeper understanding. In our dealings with Latin America, we tend to be condescending, patronizing, "superior." We tend to employ stereotypes that are not complimentary. While we usually eschew racial, ethnic, religious, and other prejudices in our public discourse about the area, privately we sometimes harbor suspicions that the stereotypes may be correct, that the Latin Americans "just aren't up to it." Since *we* are more developed economically than Latin America, we tend also to assume we are more "developed" socially, politically, intellectually, even morally. We really believe that our social and political systems are superior to theirs and that they must "learn from us."[4] Finally we, and that includes a shocking number of professional Latin Americanists, frequently harbor a quite definite hostility toward Latin America and toward the Catholic, corporate, organic, hierarchical, authoritarian, elitist, nonegalitarian, patrimonialist underpinnings on which many institutions in Latin America are based.

These often unpleasant truths concerning our attitudes toward Latin America were brought home again in the Falklands/Malvinas war of 1982, pitting Great Britain against Argentina. Our posture was not only pro-British, anti-aggression, and hence anti-Argentine, but also it was widely perceived to be anti–Latin American as well—notwithstanding the general Latin American lack of love for the Argentines. All the submerged prejudices about Latin America came out—that it is repressive, governed by quasi-fascist regimes, inherently antiliberal, anti-Semitic, antidemocratic. One had the impression of living in the sixteenth century again and of trying to present a counter or at least balanced view of the "Black Legend" of Catholic-inquisitorial-Hispanic civilization.[5] We will in the future have to live with the consequences of our actions in that crisis and of the prejudices exhibited, which seemed to confirm all the worst fears the Latin Americans harbor concerning "Anglo-Saxon" civilization.[6]

The myths we believe about Latin America and our attitudes toward it are unfortunate, but it is important also that we recognize that they do exist and deal with them realistically. Latin Americanists tend to talk mostly to each other and therefore develop a somewhat exaggerated perspective of their own area's worth and importance, a view that needs to be tempered by a broader, global overview.

At the same time, the Latin American nations themselves frequently also have an exaggerated sense of their own importance to the United States. For my own part, having batted my head against the wall of U.S. indifference, ignorance, and antipathy toward Latin America for over twenty years, with rather modest appreciable results, I think it prudent both for those in the United States interested in Latin America and for Latin Americans themselves to begin to be realistic concerning the area's place in our scheme of priorities. There will not soon be a sea change of understanding and empathy toward Latin America on the part of the general American public, nor will Latin America suddenly vault past Europe, the Soviet Union, the Middle East, or Asia in terms of our evaluation of its relative importance. Rather than simply railing against these facts, the beginning of wisdom in the policy area might be to treat them realistically and proceed from there.

The Bedrocks of U.S. Policy toward Latin America

Since approximately the turn of the century, with the Spanish-American War, the protectorates established over Cuba and Puerto Rico, and the building of the Panama Canal, which also corresponds with the emergence of the United States as a major industrial and world power, the interests of the United States in Latin America—and especially in the Caribbean Basin area—have been almost constant. It has not mattered a great deal, except in terms of emphases and nuance, which American administration was in power. The fact is there has been remarkable consistency in the bedrocks of U.S. policy toward the area over the past eighty-odd years. These historic continuities of policy are perhaps as strongly present even now as they were nearly a century ago.[7]

U.S. hegemonic interests in the area have been mainly strategic, economic, and political. These may be further subdivided in terms of *primary interests* and *secondary interests*. In outline form these may be summarized as follows:

A. *Primary Interests*

1. Maintain access to the area's raw materials, primary products, markets, and sea lanes; protection of the sea lanes and regions around the Panama Canal; protection of borders, both our own and others'.

2. Maintain stability in ways that are compatible with U.S. interests—political, economic, and strategic. Maintaining stability in this sense means not necessarily an incorrigible defense of the status quo but also incorporates adaptation to and acceptance of change on the part of the United States—but change within prescribed and acceptable boundaries.

3. Keep out hostile foreign powers. This implied actions with regard to Great Britain, France, and Spain in the nineteenth century; against Germany in World Wars I and II and between the wars; and against the Soviet Union or its agents or proxies since the onset of the cold war.

B. *Secondary Interests*

In contrast to the primary interests listed previously, which constitute the true bedrock of U.S. policy, what we have termed "secondary interests"—the defense of human rights or the defense of democracy—tend to be pursued only in noncrisis times. Some domestic U.S. groups object to this lower priority for democracy and human rights concerns; but I think history and the political record demonstrate that even the most liberal of U.S. governments—those of Franklin D. Roosevelt, John F. Kennedy, or Jimmy Carter, for instance—tend to favor democracy and human rights usually in the abstract and at the rhetorical level, and in situations of calm and "luxury" where the other first-order priorities are not pressing. When the primary interests of security, stability, and hegemony seem threatened, however, U.S. efforts to push democracy and human rights in Latin America are sidetracked or given a lower-order priority. Although some may decry these priorities, the evidence from the times of FDR, JFK, or Carter is overwhelming.

C. *Corollary*

A caveat should be introduced at this time, and that is that U.S. policy in Latin America tends to be crisis oriented. This relates to the generally low-order priority afforded the area as a whole. That is, when a crisis explodes, as in Guatemala in 1954, Cuba as it underwent revolutionary change, the Dominican Republic in 1965, Chile in the early 1970s, and more recently El Salvador and Nicaragua, we turn our attention—usually belatedly—to Latin America. The rest of the time we hope and tend to ignore it.

If one accepts, as history I think demonstrates we must, the notion that there are certain bedrocks of U.S. policy that virtually all administrations since 1898 have generally shared and on which there is widespread popular consensus, however much some professional Latin Americanists may wish to change these priorities, then it follows that there is likely to be little disagreement from American administration to administration on these basics. Indeed I wish to argue that there has been in fact little dissent for nearly a century in U.S. policy-making circles over the basics of U.S. policy toward Latin America. These bedrocks have been listed previously, and the understanding and acceptance of them are almost universal in the U.S. government and among members of both major parties. There are arguments over emphases, of course, but seldom over basics. The real argument in U.S. Latin American policy, I would suggest, has not been over the fundamental goals of U.S. policy but rather over the best and most appropriate means to achieve those goals.

Some (often labeled "realists") believe that U.S. interests as outlined here are best served by providing assistance to strong and authoritarian regimes, usually dictators or military governments, that are able vigorously and forcefully to defend public order and that are strongly, sometimes brutally, anti-Communist. Given the divisive, chaotic forces existent in Latin America, the argument runs, the best defense against national fragmentation and breakdown that might lead to a Communist takeover is a strong or strong-arm regime that keeps labor, students, and peasants "in their place" and thereby helps protect American interests.

Others (often called "idealists") believe that U.S. interests are best served by being on the side of democracy, human rights, and the "forces for change." Only in this way, the argument goes, can U.S. interests be served in the longer term. Since the oligarchies and dictators with whom we frequently ally are slated inevitably for the ashcans of history, it behooves the United States to abandon these "traditional institutions" and get on the side of the "newer forces." It is better for the United States to help lead the change process, the advocates of this position argue, than to risk being overwhelmed by it and losing all, as in Cuba during its revolution.

In my own view, both of these arguments are severely flawed because they are both based on fundamentally wrong assumptions about Latin America and its change processes. Both demonstrate a fundamental lack of understanding about Latin America, both are based on models derived chiefly from the U.S. experience, and both demonstrate a large degree of that familiar American ethnocentrism that we argued earlier was at the core of our malcomprehension of and international difficulties with the area. I have written at length on these themes and cannot repeat all those materials here.[8] Let us therefore return to the argument as seen from the point of view of U.S. policy makers.

Thus seen, U.S. policy seems to oscillate between two polar points: a "conservative" position often identified with assistance to strong governments and a "liberal" position identified with aid to the new and "democratizing" forces. Leaving aside for now the accuracy or lack thereof of these two labels or their relevance within the Latin American context, it seems clear that these two positions may also be identified with our two dominant political parties. That is, the "conservative" position is usually associated with the Republican party and the "liberal" one with the Democratic party. Allowing for various factions and different points of view within the two major parties, the point is so obvious as to constitute a truism.

The real situation, however, is both more simple and more complex than that. The following propositions begin to get at those complexities and to provide a link with our earlier analysis:

1. While our policies (and governments) often seem to oscillate between these liberal and conservative positions, in fact all recent American governments have sought to blend and reconcile these two. The Carter administration no more abandoned American security

doctrine in Latin America than the Reagan administration abandoned a concern for human rights. To be sure there are different emphases and balances that are struck, but no recent American government has even contemplated embracing the one pole of U.S. policy to the complete abandonment of the other.[9]

2. It must also be recalled that while there have been considerable disagreements over the best *means* to secure U.S. interests in the area, the *goals* have remained generally set and constant. That is, while some believe leading social change is the best way for the United States to forestall a Communist takeover and others think aid to dictators best serves that purpose, it is important to recall that both points of view have a common goal: the prevention of a hostile power or ideology from gaining dominance in the area.

3. In accord with the "lesser evil" doctrine, when given the choice between U.S. support for a wobbly, uncertain, and unstable democratic government (for example, Bosch in the Dominican Republic in 1963, Goulart in Brazil, Allende in Chile), the United States will almost always opt for the lesser evil of a stable authoritarian regime. The lesser evil doctrine is closely congruent with our division of U.S. interests into primary and secondary: we may be willing to assist a wobbly democrat in noncrisis times and in situations where our fundamental interests are not affected; but in crisis times when our primary or "bedrock" interests are affected, the lesser evil of support for stable authoritarianism is likely to be the policy pursued, whatever the particular administration in power at the moment.

4. These comments must all be considered in a context of decreasing U.S. influence throughout the hemisphere, a trend that has also continued under the administration of President Reagan. The present restraints on U.S. policy and actions make some of the earlier options increasingly difficult to carry out.

5. All these comments add up to a major conclusion, and that is the existence of far greater continuity in U.S. policy toward Latin America than we usually think. In the rhetorical flourishes that capture so many headlines and in the debate over means and emphases, we often forget that the basic goals and ends have been largely constant. Succeeding administrations have in fact demonstrated remarkable continuity in supporting the fundamental goals of U.S. policy and in arriving at some remarkable parallels in their ranking of U.S. priorities. That applies not just to the transition from JFK to Lyndon Baines Johnson but also from Presidents Carter to Reagan—as indeed it has to all U.S. administrations since the past century. Let us turn to some specific cases.

Change and Continuity in U.S. Latin American Policy

The shift from the Carter to the Reagan administration seemed to portend a radical alteration in the Latin American policy of the United States. The changes about to occur were heralded in a series of statements made during the campaign, in a variety of writings and transition team papers written by Reagan foreign policy advisers, and in many of the early statements made by Reagan administration officials.[10]

The new emphases may be summarized as follows:

1. It appeared there would now be less attention to human rights than had been the case under President Carter.

2. It seemed there would now be greater stress on the East-West conflict, rather than on the indigenous causes of Latin America's upheavals.

3. Less attention, it appeared, would now be given to public assistance and more to private investment.

4. The call was issued for more "realism" and less "idealism" in U.S. foreign policy.

5. Totalitarian leftists were now viewed as worse than authoritarian rightists. U.S. aid and favors would be redirected accordingly.

But the realities of power and the complexities of the issues facing the administration have led to a considerable moderating of these positions—so much so that one now wonders if all the rhetoric may not have been chiefly for domestic political purposes and only to a lesser degree meant to be applied to Latin America. No one would deny there have been differences between the Carter and Reagan approaches, but these were greatly exaggerated and smothered in political and campaign rhetoric. Actually, many elements of policy have remained the same, and those who say otherwise may be heard with considerable skepticism. They are often jockeying for position and advantage in the next election and/or administration, and therefore have a vested or partisan interest in emphasizing the differences at the expense of the continuities.

At this stage, therefore, one must look at what the Reagan administration has actually done or is doing and no longer at the campaign rhetoric that dominated the early debates and that some analysts still employ to serve their own political purposes. Space constraints rule out our discussing all aspects of present U.S. policy in full detail, but some major aspects may be highlighted as a way of demonstrating the continuity theme.[11]

1. *El Salvador.* El Salvador and U.S. policy there remain a controver-

sial issue that cannot here be put to rest. Nor can all the questions be adequately answered. My own assessment has been that the debate has frequently been far off base (to expect "democracy" in El Salvador may not be realistic, and to expect the El Salvadoran military to be subordinated to civilian government is equally unrealistic).[12] Specifically with regard to U.S. policy, however, the following considerations, among others, seem important: first, that a policy of military assistance to El Salvador was actually begun under Carter (as one of his last acts in office) and only continued and somewhat expanded under Reagan; second, that both administrations have sought (with uneven success) to bolster in power a moderate, civilian, reformist government; third, that both administrations sought to carry out a limited agrarian reform program (while also recognizing the difficulties of any such reforms in the midst of a civil war); fourth, that both have sought to encourage greater respect for human rights while also limiting repression and abuses; fifth, that both administrations have practiced prudence and restraint against the urging of some for full-scale U.S. military intervention. I see, in short, more continuity in U.S. policy toward El Salvador than is frequently indicated in our public discussion.

2. *Nicaragua.* Both the Carter and the Reagan administrations publicly attacked the emerging Marxism-Leninism of the Nicaraguan regime; both followed a strategy of seeking reconciliation with the Sandinista-led government on the one hand and opposing its excesses on the other; both undertook vigorous efforts to keep the revolution from spreading to neighboring countries; both expressed opposition to a greater Cuban and/or Soviet influence; both tried to encourage greater pluralism within Nicaragua; both sought to maintain diplomatic relations and influence while concurrently stepping up the economic and even military pressure. That is also a strategy of considerable continuity and not of dramatic change.

3. *Human rights.* The Carter administration received much credit for its human rights policy, inept though it often was, while the Reagan administration was criticized for the absence of such a policy. It is true that the Reagan administration tended to see human rights as a lesser priority, a "secondary interest" in our terminology. In fact, that was also true of the Carter administration however much its apologists now choose to argue otherwise. Further, a strong case could be made that the human rights accomplishments carried out quietly under Elliott Abrams in the Reagan administration have been at least as significant as those carried out noisily (and that were often self-defeating for that very reason) under Patricia Derian in the Carter administration.

4. *Caribbean Basin Initiative.* As finally formulated, after one of the most interesting processes of consultations with the recipient governments of any U.S. aid program ever, the CBI provides essentially for a combination of aid and trade and a blend of public and private initiatives. After all the early talk of U.S. efforts to export its own brand of capitalism to the Caribbean and the considerable criticism because of that emphasis, frankly the CBI in its final form looks to me remarkably similar to the Alliance for Progress propounded twenty years ago by a liberal-democratic administration. Again, the theme is continuity rather than major new departures.

5. *Cuba.* The Reagan administration conducted talks with Cuba's revolutionary government as had the Carter, Ford, and Nixon administrations before it.[13] While Cuba clearly wants the embargo lifted and wishes access to our markets, capital, and technology, it has not so far been willing to pay the costs in terms of curtailing its international adventurism in Angola, the Horn of Africa, or Central America upon which a series of U.S. administrations have insisted. Hence relations remain testy and strained. But that is hardly anything new.

6. *The Southern Cone.* The Reagan administration sought to normalize its relations with the important Southern Cone countries, while also maintaining some quieter-than-Carter pressure to return them to more democratic practices. After all the ups and downs of policy of *both* administrations in the past few years, however, relatively little seems to have changed: Chile continues to go its own authoritarian way and U.S. influence there is limited, while in Argentina in the aftermath of the Falklands/Malvinas controversy relations have returned to "normal"—that is, frosty, aloof, distant, and not a little bit distrustful.

7. *Other areas: Brazil, Mexico.* There has been at some levels a certain reconciliation on the part of the United States with Brazil and Mexico, compared with the causes for discontent in the relations that existed previously. But with these as with other countries not discussed, there are also long-term differences over a host of important issues that are also likely to continue into whatever U.S. administration follows.

In all these and other instances it is fair to say that U.S. Latin American policy has been more pragmatic, centrist, and middle-of-the-road than the campaign rhetoric and early statements of the Reagan administration would have led one to believe. Indeed much the same could be said for the preceding Carter administration: that it began with a considerable rhetorical flourish that owed something to the McGovern wing of the Democratic party and then underwent a considerable process of moderation. One should not of course ignore the importance of these early "signals," especially in Latin America. In actual fact we may be agreed there was little change in policy, but in Latin America even modest changes of emphases or of personnel from one administration to the next are often perceived as representing major shifts. It is again reflective of the low priority we assign the area, however, that in the United States we seldom are aware of or pay serious attention to these Latin American sentiments. And in any case it is quite clear that by the midpoint of the Reagan administration Latin America was receiving quite different—more pragmatic, centrist, and moderate—signals than it had received at the beginning.

Not only is there more continuity between the Carter and Reagan administrations' Latin American policies than is often thought, but also in both administrations there was, after the early rhetoric had faded, a tendency toward moderation and centrism. Furthermore in both administrations there has been, for good or ill, a rather closer fit than thought with the historical bedrocks of policy and with mainstream, domestic public opinion. The reasons both for this continuity and for the tendency toward centrism merit some attention.

Moderation and Stability in U.S. Latin American Policy

The stability and continuity of U.S. Latin American policy are quite remarkable. For nearly a hundred years that policy, obviously with variations and some new departures, has been remarkably consistent. The bedrocks of policy have been set and the boundaries of permissible and acceptable debate largely agreed upon. Within those boundaries there may be considerable debate, and as indicated there is also discussion of how best to implement the goals of policy that have been largely set. But beyond those boundaries acceptable and mainstream debate has seldom gone; nor have we been willing—as the Falklands/Malvinas crisis of 1982 illustrated—to elevate Latin America to a new priority, to pay it more than peripheral attention, or to reexamine our fundamental assessments and/or prejudices about the area.

What then are the factors explaining this remarkable stability and continuity of policy, despite the various ups and downs of which we are all also aware? I have chosen to consider this question under two categories of forces, domestic and international.

A. *Domestic Forces*

1. *The media.* The media clearly are more liberal than the Reagan administration.[14] With regard to El Salvador, for instance, the drumbeat of media coverage portraying the government and armed forces

in the harshest terms and often romanticizing the guerrillas as mere social reformers became so incessant and overwhelming that many serious foreign policy observers in Washington began to question whether the United States could ever carry out a coherent, rational foreign policy—whatever the merits of specific tactics in this particular case. For any administration concerned with its image and with public opinion, there is no doubt the coverage of El Salvador had a restraining impact. No administration can withstand a campaign that portrays it as bolstering a regime that butchers its opponents. Media coverage of these events, however biased and inaccurate at times, undoubtedly affected the administration's position.

2. *Congress.* Foreign policy analysts seldom paid it much attention in the past, but there is no doubt that Congress has become a major influence on foreign policy making.[15] Through its hearings, the deliberations over aid bills like the CBI, the process of human rights certification for countries that receive our assistance, the independent views of congressmen that are readily conveyed to the media,[16] the requirements of testimony and questionings to which administration policy makers must submit—these give the Congress considerable influence, if only as a nuisance factor. And since all policy is based on quid pro quos and trade-offs, the administration frequently finds itself paying a debt in one area for a favor in an entirely unrelated one; and Latin America, as a comparatively "unimportant" policy area, is frequently where the bargaining takes place.[17]

3. *Public opinion.* Any administration responds to the polls or the opinion "back home"—perhaps even, though it is arguable, to the resolutions of the Latin American Studies Association. Again in the case of El Salvador, public opinion was poisoned by the brutality, corruption, and atrocities attributed to the regime or its security forces. How could the administration defend any regime that massacred journalists, raped and murdered nuns, and slaughtered innocent civilians? The impact of the killing of the nuns, perhaps more important in shaping policy toward El Salvador than any other single event, was not immediately apparent to the administration; but as the brutality of the images on the television screens sank in, policy changed.

4. *Domestic politics.* The political science literature has shown that the key explanatory factor in determining how congressmen vote (and doubtless other elected officials as well) is not age, party, religion, ideology, state, or district. Rather it is the desire to be reelected.[18] Indeed one could make a strong case that U.S. Latin American policy is in its essentials a reflection of our domestic politics, that practically everything we do in Latin America is assessed not so much for its effect on that area as on our own domestic scene. The point need not

be belabored, but it is clear that U.S. domestic politics also helped mitigate our Latin American policy, particularly as first the 1982 congressional election and then the general and presidential election campaign of 1984 began.

5. *The influence of interest groups.* Big business, big labor, and now some religious and other groups in this country either run their own foreign policies often quite independently of the administration's wishes, or have become very effective as lobbying agencies. Their power is such that no administration can afford entirely to ignore them. The influence of these groups has undoubtedly served to moderate U.S. Latin American policy.

6. *The bureaucracy.* Two aspects of this phenomenon command our attention. The first is the sheer inertia and continuity within the government bureaucracy, which no new administration can entirely command or reorient in a short period. The bureaucracy tends to have a vested interest in established policies and procedures and is often far more skillful than any mere elected government at protecting its interests and preserving continuity.

The second is almost a "natural law" of new administrations. The "president's men," those who accompany him during the campaign and go with him into office, are often more ideological than the permanent government service, and during the first year of a new administration they tend to command headlines and policy making. But after that first year, bureaucratic and policy expertise, both on regional and on functional issues, gradually is reasserted. Policy is then "recaptured" by the bureaucrats, in the Department of State and elsewhere, and the ideologues are gradually supplanted. The process has recently been undertaken in part in the Reagan administration, an administration that took considerable pains to ensure programmatic and ideological consistency in all the foreign policy-making agencies: the National Security Council, the Central Intelligence Agency, the Departments of Defense and State, and the United States Information Agency.[19]

B. *International Forces*

1. *Complexity.* International situations usually prove far more complex when they must actually be dealt with, with far more ramifications and difficulties, than they appear during a domestic election campaign. In the case of Central America, for instance, the administration's heavy campaign emphasis on the East-West struggle proved, as its more sophisticated foreign policy advisers knew all along, to be only a partial explanation of the revolutionary struggles there. A more complex explanation followed that emphasized both the domestic and

the international roots of the troubles. But it takes time for policy to come to grips with these more complex realities and to deal with the ramifications not fully conceived of before. Complexity and reality have a remarkable moderating effect on policy.

2. *Intractability.* The problems of Central America are long term and intractable; no American effort will resolve them quickly or easily. Moreover any new administration in Washington learns rather quickly that the levers of power in Latin America are not so easily manipulable as it had thought initially. El Salvador again provides a case in point. It has proved very hard for the United States to identify the levers and institutions of power in that society to effect the kind of changes deemed desirable. Or else, once identified and grasped, the levers and institutions prove so fragile that they break off in our hands.

3. *International constraints.* One of the more interesting aspects of the drama in Central America—and deserving of further study— is the presence there of a variety of other outside actors that had not been present before. By this is meant not just the United States and Cuba but a number of new presences that make policy making more complex than in the past and that serve as further constraints on U.S. policy.

On the one hand there is "world public opinion," an amorphous term but one whose impact is considerable. World public opinion in this case means chiefly Western European opinion, mainly that of the socialist and social-democratic parties and movements. It is arguable that the Western Europeans are every bit as biased and ethnocentric in their views of Latin America as we have portrayed North America to be—maybe more so—and there is considerable suspicion that European views on Latin America are often a reflection more of their own domestic politics than of any sophisticated understanding of the area. Nonetheless such views have served as a restraint on what some would view as the excesses of U.S. policy.

Equally important have been the political and diplomatic roles played by a number of European, and even Latin American countries, in the Central American conflict. The Dutch, French, German, Italian, Swedish, British, and Spanish governments as well as a variety of European political parties, labor unions, trade and diplomatic missions, foundations, and other entities have all established connections and a presence that was nonexistent before. And such middle-level Latin American countries as Mexico and Venezuela have also played a major role in the Central American imbroglio. The increased presence of these new outside actors has added a complex dimension to U.S. policy in the area not there before and has served as a further restraint upon any unilateral U.S. action.

Conclusion

The emphasis in this paper has been on the continuities in U.S. Latin American policy. Beneath the campaign rhetoric that receives such undue attention and the "new directions" that every American administration seems obliged to announce, the bedrocks of U.S. attitudes and policy toward Latin America remain generally unaltered from administration to administration. Once the campaign rhetoric is stripped away and a new administration must deal with the realities of U.S. domestic politics, the force of international opinion and of other international actors, and the complexities and unfathomable depths of Latin American reality, a tempering process takes place which forces all administrations back toward some fundamental and agreed-upon bounds of policy. This is as true of the Reagan administration as it was of the Carter administration.

To stress the continuities of U.S. Latin American policy, however, should not lead us to ignore the new emphases that a new administration may advance. Such new emphases provide quite a bit of room for innovative thrusts, tilts, changes of personnel, nuance, maneuver, and tactics—to say nothing of the grist they provide for our domestic political debate as well as the signals that Latin American leaders receive from them. Even with such nudges in new directions, however, it is important to remember that the more fundamental basics of U.S. policy have, over the long run, remained remarkably constant.

Given basic American attitudes toward Latin America, the secondary and inferior position we assign the area, and the strategic, economic, and political bedrocks of U.S. policy on which all administrations have been in accord, it is probably unrealistic of us to expect very many fundamental shifts in our policy toward or perceptions of the area. There will be new emphases and nuances, but one should not really think, despite the laments of professional Latin Americanists, that the fundamental goals and means of U.S. policy will change much. We can nibble at the edges of these basics, and clearly the "majesty of facts"—massive migration of Latin Americans to the United States, spiraling political crises in the area that force their way into our consciousness, economic competition from several Latin American countries as well as financial upheavals provoked by the area's staggering international debts—will have its impact on our thinking. But even with all these portents, one doubts that U.S. attitudes and, with them, policy will be transformed in their fundamentals.

If basic policy is indeed as continuous and as difficult to alter as suggested here, then one probably ought not to have such elevated expectations as many of our students have about "changing the system." We may work to change the emphases, but we should probably have no grand illusions about the effect of our "getting involved." What one can perhaps realistically hope for, echoing an argument made earlier by Paul Sigmund,[20] is some greater consistency, competence, and pragmatism between administrations rather than, in his terms, an "extended morality play," with either repressive governments in one administration and the Soviet Union in the next playing the role of "devil."

Both Presidents Carter and Reagan found, as had Presidents Kennedy and Johnson before them, that neither exuberant idealism nor military force was sufficient by itself. Both rediscovered (and actually knew all along) that some balance must be achieved over time between our desire for democratic and representative governments in Latin America and our need to maintain decent relations even with regimes of which we may disapprove. Both came to see the desirability of reconciling and combining the diverse means we may use to carry out policy (aid to dictators versus aid to democrats), while also adjusting somewhat the goals and fundamental ends we seek to achieve, depending on times, circumstances, and the need to accommodate both to our own altered position in the world and to the realities of a changed, stronger, more diverse, and more independent Latin America.

Notes

1. A more detailed discussion of these themes is in Howard J. Wiarda, "Power and Policy-Making in Washington in the Latin America Area: Impressions and Reflections," Paper presented at the Center for International Affairs, Harvard University, April 20, 1982.

2. An example is our human rights campaign, but there are many others; see Howard J. Wiarda, ed., *Human Rights and U.S. Human Rights Policy* (Washington, D.C.: American Enterprise Institute, 1982).

3. *Strength through Wisdom: A Critique of United States Capabilities—A Report to the President from the President's Commission on Foreign Languages and International Studies* (Washington, D.C.: Government Printing Office, 1979).

4. A more extended treatment is in Howard J. Wiarda, ed., *The Continuing Struggle for Democracy in Latin America* (Boulder, Colo.: Westview Press, 1980).

5. R. Bruce McColm, *El Salvador: Peaceful Revolution or Armed Struggle?* (New York: Freedom House, 1982); Mark Falcoff, "The Apple of Discord: Central America in U.S. Domestic Politics," in Howard J. Wiarda, ed., *Rift and Revolution: The Central American Imbroglio* (Washington, D.C.: American Enterprise Institute, 1984).

6. Howard J. Wiarda, "The United States and Latin America in the After-

math of the Falklands/Malvinas Crisis," Testimony prepared for the Subcommittee on Inter-American Affairs, Committee on Foreign Affairs, U.S. House of Representatives, July 20, 1982; chapter 2 in this volume.

7. The first influential and comprehensive treatment—and one that still has relevance—is by Alfred Thayer Mahan, *The Interest of America in Sea Power, Present and Future*, reprint of 1891 ed. (New York: Kennikat Press, Inc., 1970). See also Margaret Daly Hayes, "U.S. National Security Interests in Global Perspective," in Richard S. Feinberg, ed., *Central America: The International Dimensions of the Crisis* (New York: Holmes and Meier, 1982).

8. Howard J. Wiarda, *Corporatism and National Development in Latin America* (Boulder, Colo.: Westview Press, 1981); idem, *Politics and Social Change in Latin America: The Distinct Tradition*, 2d rev. ed. (Amherst: University of Massachusetts Press, 1982).

9. These and other arguments are elaborated in Wiarda, *Rift and Revolution*, a book-length study of Central America to be published by AEI and containing essays by the present author, Jeane Kirkpatrick, Gary Wynia, Ronald H. McDonald, Roland Ebel, Ernest Evans, Jiri and Virginia Valenta, Mark Falcoff, Thomas Anderson, Eusebio Mujal-León, Thomas Karnes, and Edward J. Williams.

10. Jeane Kirkpatrick, "Dictatorships and Double Standards," *Commentary*, vol. 70 (November 1979), pp. 34–45; Constantine Menges, "Central America and Its Enemies," *Commentary*, vol. 72 (August 1981), pp. 32–38; Roger Fontaine, Cleto Di Giovanni, Jr., and Alexander Kruger, "Castro's Specter," *Washington Quarterly*, vol. 3 (Autumn 1980), pp. 3–27; James D. Theberge et al., *Latin America: Struggle for Progress* (Lexington, Mass.: Lexington Books, 1976); Pedro A. Sanjuan, "Why We Don't Have a Latin America Policy," *Washington Quarterly*, vol. 3 (Autumn 1980), pp. 28–39; and The Committee of Santa Fe, Lewis Tambs, ed., *A New Inter-American Policy for the Eighties* (Washington, D.C.: Council for Inter-American Security, 1980).

11. The emphasis on continuity has also been stressed by Paul Sigmund, "Latin America: Change or Continuity," *Foreign Affairs*, vol. 60, no. 3 (1981), pp. 629–57; Susan Kaufman Purcell, "Carter, Reagan et l'Amerique Centrale," *Politique Etrangère*, vol. 47 (June 1982), pp. 309–17; and Abraham F. Lowenthal, "Ronald Reagan and Latin America: Coping with Hegemony in Decline," in Kenneth A. Oye et al., *Eagle Defiant: United States Foreign Policy in the 1980s* (Boston: Little, Brown, 1983), pp. 311–35. See also the remarks by Assistant Secretary of State for Inter-American Affairs Thomas O. Enders, "Building the Peace in Central America," The Commonwealth Club, San Francisco, August 20, 1982.

12. See the discussion in "The Crisis in Central America," special issue of the *AEI Foreign Policy and Defense Review*, vol. 4, no. 2 (1982), Howard J. Wiarda, guest editor.

13. Wayne Smith, "Dateline Havana: Myopic Diplomacy," *Foreign Policy*, no. 48 (Fall 1982), pp. 157–74. Although in the press coverage of this article Smith's criticisms of the Reagan administration initiatives received most attention, the article itself was equally critical of the Carter policies.

14. A serious, scholarly study based on interviewing of the principals is S. Robert Lichter and Stanley Rothman, "Media and Business Elites," *Public Opinion*, vol. 4 (October/November 1981), pp. 42–46, 59–60.

15. Robert A. Pastor, *Congress and the Politics of U.S. Foreign Economic Policy, 1929 to 1976* (Berkeley: University of California Press, 1980).

16. One of the more interesting Washington phenomena is the rise of former Peace Corps volunteers, such as Senators Dodd and Tsongas of the Foreign Relations Committee, into positions of influence where their quite independent and Peace Corps–shaped views carry major weight.

17. This process and others are discussed in Wiarda, "Power and Policy-Making in Washington."

18. David R. Mayhew, *Congress: The Electoral Connection* (New Haven, Conn.: Yale University Press, 1974).

19. Lowenthal, "Ronald Reagan"; also Enders, "Building the Peace."

20. Sigmund, "Latin America."

4

Pluralism in Nicaragua?

The Department of State needs to conceptualize.
—Henry Kissinger

My assignment in this symposium was to focus on "the prospects for political pluralism in Nicaragua." In keeping with the admonition of the former secretary of state, I wish to approach this issue theoretically and conceptually. My purpose is not so much to provide an updated factual assessment of the Nicaraguan situation, which others in the symposium and the Department of State itself can do quite adequately. Rather my purpose is to provide a framework in which Nicaraguan pluralism and its prospects can be analyzed and assessed.

What Pluralism Means in That Context

To begin with, pluralism in Nicaragua, historically, should be thought of as different from that of the United States. As distinct from the untrammeled, virtual laissez-faire pluralism of the United States, pluralism in Nicaragua has always been more limited. Whether under the old regime or under the new, this form of limited pluralism implies a limited number of groups competing in the political arena and limited freedom for them. These groups operate under a variety of official restraints, they are subject to a far greater degree than their American counterparts to state controls, and they function within a state-society arena in which the authoritarian state and not the "society" has long been predominant. Within this context it may be unreasonable to expect a system of free associability, untrammeled competitiveness, and a balanced interest-group structure to develop. Limited pluralism is the norm rather than the exception; even in the best of circumstances, a system of limited pluralism may be all that could be expected.

Presented at the Department of State, Washington, D.C.; February 12, 1982; published in *Papers Presented at a Conference on Nicaragua* (Washington, D.C.: Department of State, 1982).

A second and related feature is that all these groups tend to be dependent on the state for largess, licensing, and their very existence. This further impedes their independence and their effectiveness. It also implies that their political relations tend to be directly with the central state and seldom with each other. They are dependent on the state for jobs, favors, contracts, permits, positions, even the right to function. Dependence on the state was the norm before the revolution, and it has become even more so since then with more and more concentrated power, to say nothing of the inheritance by the state of the old Somoza properties. This gives the central state enormous regulatory and controlling power while at the same time retarding the possibilities for the building of crosscutting loyalties or intergroup alliances. All groups tend to look individually to the state for guidance, direction, access, and almost all economic and political opportunities. Their capacity to resist state direction, either singularly or in alliance with other groups, is hence quite limited. These arenas of state-society relations are critical for understanding Nicaraguan political behavior, but in the present context it must be emphasized that it is the state that is overwhelmingly dominant while the societal groups play a weaker, perhaps even subservient role.

Third, one must bear in mind the nature of the overall Latin American change process and the place of Nicaragua within this framework. The traditional, accommodative model of Latin American change implies the gradual incorporation of new social and political groups into the system provided two conditions are met: (1) the new groups must demonstrate a sufficient power capability (through elections, mass mobilizations, street action, and the like) to be perceived as a threat to the status quo and therefore deserving of admission to the system; and (2) they must indicate a willingness to abide by the prevailing system's rules of the game, which must include the assurance that the traditional ruling groups will not be entirely eliminated from power. Failure by the traditional ruling groups to accommodate the newer groups even though they have met and agreed to these preconditions may—and in Nicaragua did—give rise to an alternative model of Latin American change, the revolutionary one. And the triumph of a new challenger through revolutionary means—again, as in Nicaragua—implies that the revolutionaries in power need not follow the rules of the accommodative model: that is, they need not abide by the understanding that the traditional groups should not be destroyed.

It is this dynamic, this tension, that lies at the heart of the present discussion concerning the prospects for political pluralism in Nicaragua. The old regime had failed to accommodate and adjust sufficiently to absorb the new and rising groups; its intransigence and unwillingness to allow sufficiently for social and political change helped precipitate the revolutionary uprising aimed at its overthrow. And now that the old regime has been overthrown and the Sandinistas have emerged triumphant, the urge and need to restrain or even eliminate the traditional wielders of power are strong.

The fact is that in Nicaragua at present both models, the accommodative and the revolutionary, continue to coexist, although the relative balance between them has shifted over time. On the one hand there has been a clear diminution in the power of the traditional groups (the Church, the business community, the press, the professional associations), but it is also the case that as yet they have not been entirely destroyed or replaced by monolithic state-run agencies. On the other hand, while the Sandinistas have moved to consolidate and strengthen their hold on power, they do not yet monopolize it entirely in totalitarian fashion.

A fourth point regarding Nicaraguan pluralism flows from the above. Pluralism in a revolutionary regime means something different from pluralism in a liberal and democratic regime. In the latter, pluralism is open, in theory if not always in fact, to all groups. But in the former, pluralism is limited to those groups that support the revolution. Pluralism must be *within* the revolution and not outside of it. Considerable freedom may be allowed those groups that are part of the "revolutionary family"; repressive measures may be carried out against those groups deemed not sufficiently supportive. The Nicaraguan leadership has often wavered between these two forms of pluralism with, again, the tendency more toward the revolutionary model of pluralism and away from the liberal one.

Given these rival and conflicting tendencies, it is not surprising that the debate over pluralism in Nicaragua has revolved around two distinct and quite opposed interpretations. One group stresses that pluralism remains vibrant and alive in Nicaragua. The other argues that pluralism has been eliminated and replaced by a totalitarian Marxist-Leninist regime. I would like to suggest a third interpretation, and that is the high degree of sheer confusion that reigns. I am willing to concede that some degree of pluralism yet exists in Nicaragua, as indicated in the discussion that follows. At the same time there have been disturbing trends toward the consolidation of a more monolithic Marxist-Leninist regime. Perhaps, however, a more accurate assessment would also emphasize the chaos and confusion that exist, the lack of clear ideas about where and how to proceed, the fear of failure that underlies the assertive bluster. Nicaragua today is strongly characterized by disorganization, government agencies that do not function effectively, and an absence of able leaders, plans, and coherence. Uncertainty as much as certainty marks the political process, with strong pressures coming from all directions, and no clear idea of where it will all lead.

Does Pluralism Exist and Where?

It is naive, in my view, to so romanticize the Nicaraguan Revolution as to be blind to the forces at work there or to seek to minimize what can only be described as dangerous currents. The steps taken to reduce political pluralism in Nicaragua have been many, cumulative, and perhaps irreversible; the other side of this coin is the growing concentration of power in the hands of Marxist-Leninist elements within the Sandinista regime. At the same time, one should not, in my view, write off as yet the entire Nicaraguan Revolution as wholly monolithic and totalitarian in the Soviet or Cuban mold. There appears to be still some room for maneuver, though the possibilities for such have narrowed, and there are ominous signs (the massive military buildup, resettlement of the Misquito Indians, greater restrictions on press activity, clampdown on opposition and labor elements, stronger Sandinista dominance) that they may narrow further or constrain altogether any possibilities for pluralism. Wishful thinking in this regard can be no substitute for hard analysis.

The prospects for political pluralism, and with it the prospects for maneuver and political diversity within the regime, may be discussed at three levels. First, at the state level, political pluralism has been reduced most significantly. The trends in this direction are clear and need not be extensively discussed here. Within the state-administrative agencies of the revolutionary government, there has been a clear trend toward (1) increasing Sandinista dominance and (2) within that, increasing dominance by hard-line Marxist-Leninist elements. The degree of pluralism within the regime and the state machinery has thus been considerably reduced since the early months of the revolution. Those in the field are in a better position to judge precisely which agencies and offices within the government, and at what levels or in what subdivisions within these agencies, are still committed to pluralist principles or retain a plurality and diversity of viewpoints— or the specific individuals within these agencies holding to pluralist principles or who themselves represent other than *oficialista* viewpoints. But the ranks of such individuals and agencies seem to be shrinking, and pluralism within the regime itself has been significantly diminished in recent months. The trends toward monism as distinct from pluralism also make it difficult for the United States to exercise much leverage vis-à-vis the regime.

Second, at the societal level somewhat greater pluralism exists. By "society" in Nicaragua we mean those groups *organized* to promote and defend their interests. Such organized groups include the Church, the press, labor, and business groups. But here too the pressures to reduce or eliminate pluralism are intense and, apparently, growing. A number of once-independent agencies are being converted into official appendages of the regime, part of the bureaucratic machinery of the state, absorbed into the regime rather than operating independently from it. Others have had their autonomy significantly reduced by an increasingly powerful and more monolithic state; still others have seen the handwriting on the wall and have been greatly reduced in strength as their members left for exile, became "apolitical," or made common cause with the prevailing winds.

Nor should one overstate the strength of those societal groups still functioning with some degree of independence from the regime. The business community has been weakened, and it is internally divided. The regime seems committed to maintaining some sectors of the economy in private hands, but that is not to say it will continue to permit an *organized* business community to speak with a strong and independent voice. The jailing and harassment of business leaders in 1982 would seem to bear out this contention.

The Church still retains its independence and offers some hopes for greater pluralism; but it is not a strong voice organizationally, it is woefully understaffed, it has little institutional strength (in hospitals and schools, for example), it is heavily dependent on foreign clergy and therefore runs the risk of being labeled antinational or anti-Nicaraguan, it has little economic influence, and therefore cannot back up its moral pronouncements with much concrete strength. Its moral suasion is considerable, and the Church does offer some possibilities as a voice for a more pluralist solution, but one should caution against excessive optimism or overreliance upon an institution that itself may be of limited strength. The press (or parts thereof) has also maintained some degree of independence, but it too is not strong and is under enormous pressure to conform to the official line or else it may simply be taken over or forced out of business.

The lines between the state and societal levels, especially among those groups that support the revolution, have become increasingly blurred. Power is concentrated in the hands of a nine-man directorate of the ruling Sandinista National Liberation Front, whose members have become both more and more hard-line and more and more unified on policy matters. Below the nine is the Sandinista party, of about 4,500 members, which offers guidance and policy directives to local, provincial, and national government officials. Alongside and often overlapping with the party is a network of labor, peasant, neighborhood and other organizations supported by government funds and other backing, which therefore have been able to compete successfully against a shrinking number of non-Sandinista organizations. Not only do the revolutionary groups enjoy official support, but as the government's line has hardened, the regime has been less inclined to listen to and accommodate the non-Sandinista groups.[1]

At the third level, general public opinion, considerably greater pluralism exists. Sentiment favoring a national or *Nicaraguan* solution is almost universal, sentiment which may still offer a brake on Nicaragua's becoming a Soviet satellite. At the popular level, furthermore, there is a considerable diversity of sentiments and ideologies: Christian-democratic, social-democratic, independent Marxist, liberal-democratic, and others. The problem is that this sentiment is inchoate, lacks an organizational base, and is therefore not a readily mobilizable or effective check on the regime. Moreover the regime itself is making strenuous efforts, through the educational system and other avenues, to enforce ideological conformity on the general population. Public sentiment remains more pluralistic than the regime itself, and such sentiment may be nurtured; but whether that offers a large degree of hope for a more pluralist political system remains problematic.

There are, thus, necessary distinctions and differing assessments that must be made between the political pluralism of the state, the pluralism of society, and the pluralism of the general population. One could probably also make the case that these sectors have been listed above in orders of descending rank with regard to their degree or level of pluralism, that the closer one comes to the regime and the machinery of the central state, the less pluralistic it appears. That is, the general population is still more open to plural views and a diversity of perspectives than are the major societal groups, and the latter in turn remain somewhat more pluralistic than the state-administrative system. It should be said that this situation is in accord with that of other revolutionary regimes in their early stages of consolidation, as discussed in the general literature.

To these distinctions must be added another: the degree to which the pluralism that still exists in Nicaragua is genuine or only *para Inglés ver*—in this instance clearly "for the Americans and Europeans to see." There is no doubt in other areas the Cubans and other advisers have been telling the Nicaraguan revolutionaries not to go too fast at first, not to antagonize the United States to the point of final rupture, not to scare off its educated *técnico* and entrepreneurial elements whom the regime sorely needs, not to alienate public opinion and support abroad. Part of this strategy has been, therefore, to retain some freedom of action and a degree of independence for non-Sandinista elements, specifically in the press and the business sector. Hence the degree to which the pluralism that remains in Nicaragua reflects genuine freedom and autonomy for these groups, or if it is only a fa™ade designed to influence favorably foreign attitudes and therefore open to future manipulation or perhaps even elimination, is not entirely clear. But the implications of these comments are certainly worrisome.

Conclusions and Implications

One should not expect pluralism to exist in Nicaragua to the same degree as it does in the United States, and certainly in the present revolutionary context the possibilities for a free and unfettered system of associability are unlikely. At best what one may hope for is a system of limited, controlled, and quite regulated pluralism. Even in the best of circumstances, therefore, it seems unrealistic to expect that Nicaragua might fashion a system of free-wheeling or laissez-faire pluralism since that runs counter to both its entire history and political tradition and is also at odds with the orientation of its present revolutionary regime.

There remains some degree of pluralism in Nicaragua, more at the popular level than at the societal level, more at the societal level than at the level of the state machinery—but not entirely absent even there. One would be naive, however, not to admit that the level and degrees of pluralism have been significantly reduced in the past two years, or that they could not be reduced still further or eliminated altogether. The fate of political pluralism in Nicaragua seems to me exceedingly precarious.

The fact that pluralism has been reduced also implies a lessening—short of stronger diplomatic or military means—in the capacity of the United States to have an impact on the revolution and to help influence its direction. There remains some room for maneuver and negotiations, but this appears to be growing more constrained. Nicaragua is still heavily dependent on the United States in various ways, and the Soviet Union does not appear eager to supply the same level of massive funding it does to Cuba. This gives the United States some considerable economic and political leverage and bargaining power vis-à-vis the regime. The sheer confusion that exists in the country also provides some room for maneuver and political bargaining. But the decline of pluralism in Nicaragua has the important political implication that the means available to us to help shape the structure of Nicaragua's internal revolution and influence its foreign policy are limited.

Note

1. The analysis has been enriched by a major feature article in the *Washington Post*, June 15, 1983.

5

U.S. Policy and the Certification of Progress in El Salvador

The debate over U.S. policy in Central America, and now specifically with regard to the presidential certification of progress in El Salvador, has been long, arduous, increasingly tumultuous—and often unfocused, unsatisfactory, and more a reflection of U.S. domestic politics than of the realities of Central America.

On the one side are lined up various human rights groups, dedicated and sincere though not necessarily representative of mainstream public opinion, who often unfortunately have little in-depth knowledge of El Salvador and whose criteria of human rights are sometimes so pristine as to be entirely unrealizable in the real world, certainly in the El Salvadoran one and most likely even in the United States. One sympathizes with the goals of a vigorous human rights policy while also wondering about the standards set and whether there are not other American interests to which we ought also to give attention.

On the other side is the administration, whose policy is under assault and whose efforts to certify progress in difficult countries like El Salvador lead to disputes, unsatisfying arguments over terms and figures, mutual suspicions, and considerable hyperbole. One group posits standards that are all but impossible to meet; the other is forced to argue that El Salvador is in the process of becoming "just like us"— which it assuredly is not. Where in all this posturing and verbal overkill is there room for a sound, reasonable, and prudent course on which some coherent policy consensus can be based?

A good beginning point for the discussion is a recognition that the social and political processes of a country like El Salvador do not always conform to our norms—neither those of the human rights groups nor the same categories often used in response by the administration. In this confusion and circumlocution, the certification process and presumptions themselves sometimes seem part of the trou-

Presented before the Committee on Foreign Relations, United States Senate, February 2, 1983; published in *Presidential Certification on Progress in El Salvador: Hearings before the Committee on Foreign Relations, United States Senate* (Washington, D.C.: GPO, 1983).

ble—but that is another story. We need to understand El Salvador realistically and on its own terms, not just through U.S. lenses.

Second, what is required is a policy that is true to our values and interests, that provides policy makers and politicians with some realistic handles they can grasp, and that offers a balanced and politically acceptable perspective on events in El Salvador. It is difficult not just morally but also politically, let us recognize, to support any regime that rapes and murders nuns and others. Yet it is a regime we feel we cannot abandon for fear of a Fidelista-style takeover.

The dilemma in our policy toward El Salvador is remarkably similar to that faced by John F. Kennedy in the Dominican Republic in 1961. The president said:

> There are three possibilities in descending order of importance: a decent democratic regime, a continuation of the Trujillo regime, or a Castro regime. We ought to aim at the first, but we really cannot renounce the second until we are sure that we can avoid the third.[1]

With only the names changed, that is precisely the problem we face in El Salvador.

It is my purpose to try to provide a more realistic analysis of El Salvador, based on a long-time study of that nation's political processes, and also a set of policy recommendations that are prudent, moderate, politically acceptable, and that take account of the difficult choices we must make.

El Salvador

For policy to be successful, it must be based on realistic understandings of countries like El Salvador. A number of human rights groups have erected a Procrustean bed of idealistic standards based almost exclusively on the U.S. model. Ethnocentrism is also alive and well in the U.S. government. Both approaches blur the realities of El Salvador. Let us try to summarize briefly only some of the features that Americans find difficult to grasp.[2]

1. *A political culture of violence.* Like Cuba historically, El Salvador has had a long tradition of political violence.[3] The tradition stretches back long before the present crisis. The country has had more deaths per capita from political violence than any other country in Latin America; *machetismo,* or the butchering of one's personal and political foes, is a way of life. Such endemic, persistent violence is very diffi-

cult for Americans to understand or come to grips with. The entire political culture—governance, challenges to it, the circulation of new and old groups in and out of power—is based on the display and use of violence. We may not condone such violence, but we cannot wish it away. In this context, statements such as those in the press recently that we cannot certify El Salvador until there is "not one single death from violence" are entirely unrealistic.

2. *Civil-military relations.* It is also difficult for Americans to understand that civil-military relations in El Salvador are fundamentally different from those in the United States. First, there is no strict separation between the civilian and the military spheres, and there is widespread legitimacy for military involvement in politics. Second, the military is a distinct institution, separate from and not necessarily inferior to civilian authority legally and constitutionally, with its own rules as well as courts. No mere civilian court can expect to have jurisdiction over the military especially in conditions of civil war; nor can any mere civilian government expect to control military activities entirely. When we condemn human rights abuses by "the government" of El Salvador, therefore, we must be careful to distinguish between the civilian and the military spheres since they are not necessarily the same, between the various services and factions within the military, and between the regular military and the several paramilitary and "uncontrollable" forces. Blanket condemnations of the whole government or the whole military are likely to be self-defeating, since they are viewed as insults and demeaning of the national honor and they force those opposed to abuses to come to the defense of their colleagues.

3. *Democracy and elections.* Democracy and elections are relative terms in El Salvador, not absolutes. They convey tentative legitimacy, not a definitive "right to rule" for a given period. Nor are democracy and elections viewed as the only route to power; coups and revolutions, in a political culture of violence, can also achieve legitimacy. The political process is therefore fluid and ongoing: witness both the U.S. efforts to modify the 1982 election results by isolating and bypassing conservative leader Roberto D'Aubuisson and the *pronunciamiento,* issued by Major Sigifredo Ochoa in January 1983. Highly moralistic arguments about democracy versus authoritarianism are not always useful for understanding these dynamics, nor are the senti ments in favor of subordinating the military to civilian authority always helpful in comprehending the murkier and mixed solutions that the El Salvadorans themselves have a genius for improvising.

4. *Human rights.* Human rights frequently mean different things in

El Salvador and in the United States.[4] There are of course universal criteria of human rights, but there are also culturally distinct nuances and meanings. Moreover there are in distinct cultures different levels of importance accorded the laws relating to human rights and also different kinds of human rights—political, social, economic, of the human person (the last being the most universal and hence for which one might have the greatest expectations of achieving success). These distinctions are seldom acknowledged in our discussions of human rights. We need to know, therefore, how and when and with what implications El Salvador violates *its own* criteria of human rights as well as when it violates our own or universal standards. When that country or its government goes beyond the pale by its own standards (as sometimes distinct from ours), then we know that government is likely to be in trouble—for example, the Somoza regime in its later years.

5. *Legal processes.* Here, too, differences are great and the potential for lack of comprehension is significant. El Salvador is a code law country, as distinct from our common law tradition; and the political and legal implications of that difference are major.[5] Nor is it possible in El Salvador to insulate the judicial process from politics or from intimidation in a general political culture of violence. In part, these factors help explain the terrible frustrations American groups and families have frequently experienced when trying to ensure that justice is carried out in some notable and tragic instances.

6. *Land and other reforms.* It is difficult to carry out a coherent agrarian reform in El Salvador in the midst of civil war. Even more basic, the distinction between private- and public-regardingness in various policy areas in that country is never so clear-cut as we presume it to be in the United States. Only when the private "house" is secure and in order can the public purposes be served. That statement, admittedly exaggerated, carries major implications for what we can and cannot reasonably expect in various public policy areas to emanate from the El Salvadoran government.

These comments, which obviously require greater refinement and elaboration than is possible here, help place the El Salvadoran political process in context. They are offered not to excuse or justify the present system there but to enable us to understand it better. Sound policy can be based only on sound understanding, on El Salvador's own terms and in its own context, of these processes at work. To this point, however, policy prescriptions have tended to be based on ethnocentric notions. I would hope a deeper comprehension could be achieved.

Policy Options: The Present Situation and Some New Realities

The present situation in El Salvador is exceedingly tense. The guerrillas seem again to be on the offensive and to be scoring some gains. To them a "gain" can be defined minimally as maintaining the status quo, from which the United States will almost certainly tire.

The armed forces have been fragmented and weakened by the *pronunciamiento* of Major Ochoa and other centrifugal forces. The military officers' meaning of "professionalism" remains different from our own. Their expectations of their roles as military officers and in El Salvadoran society are also at variance with ours.

The political system is also exceedingly shaky. The government enjoys tenuous legitimacy. Political parties and other institutions are very weak. The depressed economy adds to the troubles. A strong center has not emerged. Serious questions must be asked about how flexible the El Salvadoran system is, how much more pressure it can take before it disintegrates, how pure must it be before it satisfies our sometimes rarefied notions of proper behavior. Under even greater American pressure a further unraveling and disintegration of that system, both civilian and military—with all the Saigon-like potential for disaster that implies—is not a remote possibility.

I see five possibilities.[6] Few of them are very attractive, but some are less attractive than others. Few offer great hope of a finally happy solution, but some offer greater hopes than others. The El Salvador case is one where we must choose not between ethical good and ethical bad but among lesser evils. Even then, the chances of success are not overly great. The present course is fraught with actual and potential dangers and possible missteps. Unfortunately, from the point of view of the administration and of much U.S. public opinion, the alternatives seem even worse.

The five possibilities are

1. *Military victory of the guerrilla left.* But the guerrillas have not demonstrated that they enjoy widespread support, of peasants, workers, or others. The guerrillas were repudiated in the 1982 election. They are having trouble finding new recruits and have had to rely in part on intimidation and impressment. They have few permanent or effective bases in the countryside or in urban areas. They have won few significant military victories. Their capacity to govern is unproved The guerrillas have been stalemated and to some degree isolated. And "another Cuba in the Caribbean" would not be acceptable to this administration or, likely, some other. The guerrilla left's only

chances for success depend upon the United States' pulling out, or its inclusion in a coalition as a result of possibility 2.

2. *"Political solution" or "negotiated settlement."* This is an attractive option because it promises to end the war and get the United States out quickly. But that promise, while politically attractive, may not be realistic. It assumes that an acceptable formula can be found that will enable the United States to get out soon—when in fact it may require years for the United States to extricate itself. It also assumes that the present institutions do not enjoy considerable legitimacy and that they can be easily replaced; it further gives the guerrillas a place in the system they have not heretofore shown they deserve, by electoral mandate or other demonstrated support. It overestimates the possibilities for compromise in El Salvador or that a "negotiated settlement" is possible and workable in such a violent, fractured, and embittered society. Witness the situation in Lebanon and the difficulties of policy there; why should we assume El Salvador and Central America will be any less difficult?

The formulas put forth for a "negotiated settlement" usually exaggerate the possibility for separating the democratic left from the Marxist-Leninist left, for drawing the former into a coalition while isolating the latter, even that there *is* a viable democratic left in El Salvador. Moreover such a "settlement" would likely only represent a temporary respite in the war and would surely lead to renewed violence and more civil strife, in which the left would be in a better position than now to seize power. Such a "political solution" especially if imposed from the outside would itself be highly unstable, necessitating greater outside interference and likely degenerating again into chaos and civil war. Should that happen and El Salvador disintegrate further, it might call forth an American involvement even greater than that at present. This option has a superficial attractiveness, but it invites as many future problems—perhaps more—as it resolves.

3. *Continuation of present policies, involving consolidation and expansion of the center.* This is, at present, the most desired U.S. outcome, from the point of view of the administration. But it assumes that there is an El Salvadoran center (both civilian and military), that the armed forces can be reformed, that the center political parties (that is, the Christian Democrats) can be reconstituted, that moderate and willing leaders can be found, that viable reforms can be effectively carried out, that the war effort can be successfully pursued. These are all big assumptions. None may work out.

Nevertheless this option provides several straws to hang on to. It offers some hope, and there are encouraging signs. We will never get the El Salvadoran military out of politics, but there are indications it now sees the bigger picture. The elites are so scared of the guerrillas that they are willing to listen and bend. Major D'Aubuisson and his ultrarightist friends have been neutralized to some degree. The centrist-reformist Christian Democrats are making a comeback and establishing new ties with the peasants. New elections have been scheduled. The existing political system is not well institutionalized; but it has not fallen apart, and there are signals of increased viability and legitimacy. One cannot be overly optimistic, but there are tendencies that can be coaxed along over the long run.

These trends enable us to exercise influence in a positive and constructive way. They build in a needed reward system for improved conditions. And they give us time and possibilities. That is not a lot, nor does it constitute a great vision. But it does provide a handle and something to work with. And it does seem better than the other alternatives. It is also the most difficult option to carry out.

4. *The status quo ante*—that is, a reactionary military regime or rule by the oligarchy. Some critics would argue that this is what exists at present. In fact, the possibilities for a *real* right-wing takeover are stronger than those posed by the left. Such a regime would negate or roll back all the reforms accomplished so far. It would likely be unacceptable to the American public and to Congress. Its assistance would dry up. It would polarize El Salvador to a degree that does not exist at present. It would leave the country isolated and ostracized. A reactionary throwback of this sort has been rather consistently opposed by successive administrations.

5. *Military victory by the right*. It seems unlikely the El Salvadoran military by itself can win such total victory. The costs are prohibitive, and who would pay? The United States seems unlikely to commit its own ground forces to El Salvador in ways that would ensure victory. Even should it do so, victory may be elusive. The guerrillas would fade away rather than face defeat—only to return later. The problems of stability and legitimacy would not be resolved. And there would be major domestic political repercussions of a greater U.S. military involvement.[7]

Policy Recommendations

The problems in El Salvador are complex. There is no easy way out. There may not be any lights at the end of the El Salvadoran tunnel.

The present course seems uncertain and may not work. But in general it seems better than the other main alternatives, a guerrilla takeover or a real, unmitigated right-wing regime. If one thinks that El Salvador is in bad shape now, consider the alternatives of a real fascist government that seeks to turn the clock back and loses all popular support. Or of a guerrilla takeover that allies itself with Cuba and Nicaragua, spreads further upheaval to Honduras and Guatemala, becomes another economic basket case like Haiti, and sends streams of hundreds of thousands of refugees toward the United States by way of already overburdened Mexico.

One cannot be sanguine about the prospects. I think we must continue to try to find and support moderate and centrist elements in El Salvador. They do exist, but they are not well organized and are often unwilling to serve in public capacities. Whether such a center can be created in the long run, however, is open to question. But it is worth continuing to try.

However the process must be kept open. I think the United States is presently overcommitted in El Salvador; I think the U.S. embassy's efforts to play essentially a proconsular role may well prove self-defeating; and I have considerable faith in the capacity of El Salvadorans to find some indigenous formula or ad hoc series of solutions to their own problems, often quite independent of U.S. actions.

It is not an easy decision, but on balance I think we must stay the course in El Salvador—at least for now. Option 3 still seems to be the best and most hopeful policy. We must continue assistance—at least for now. And I think we must certify—at least for now. It is the only government that exists in El Salvador; it is to a certain extent a government of our creation, the abandonment of which would have severe repercussions; and the other alternatives seem even less acceptable. I do not believe we can abruptly abdicate our capacity to exercise influence in El Salvador.

Nevertheless policy must respect the weight of facts. It is unlikely that U.S. domestic political pressures will permit many more certifications of the El Salvadoran government in its present form. The internal reforms the administration hopes for in El Salvador (military professionalization, the reorganization of the center, agrarian and other reforms, a more effective government) may prove to be phantoms. The left in El Salvador may demonstrate a sufficient power capability that the armed forces and the right may feel a need to reach an accommodation with it.

I believe that the certification should be approved but that it should be made conditional and that we must be prepared to be flexible. The United States should begin to reduce its presence in that beleaguered country. At the same time, U.S. diplomacy and initiatives should be undertaken to ensure that other outside forces cannot meddle in El Salvador's internal affairs.

Then, should the main props of the U.S. strategy begin to crumble, should the El Salvadoran military not prove reformable, the center not emerge, the reforms be frustrated, the government prove ineffective, and should the left demonstrate greater strength than anticipated, the United States should be prepared realistically to adjust. At that stage, option 2, a negotiated settlement or a political compromise, will have to be reexamined. There are a variety of avenues, including some new initiatives emanating from Mexico, which now appears to be offering itself as an intermediary in a quieter and more acceptable fashion than in the past. Or it may be that El Salvador will have to resolve some of its own problems in its own ways, with a somewhat more limited hovering presence by the United States. Or the United States may combine talks with continued efforts to strengthen El Salvador's government and armed forces.

In all these considerations it is facts not romance that must govern our decisions. We must not romanticize the guerrillas or the idea of a "negotiated settlement"; at the same time the administration cannot romanticize the presumed "progress" of the El Salvadoran regime. Hard reality, pragmatism, and continued adjustment and fine-tuning of policy are necessary. In the meantime, it behooves us to reexamine both the assumptions of many aspects of our overall Latin American policy[8] *and* the assumptions and requirements of this certification process, which seems in many ways to be unsatisfactory.

Notes

1. Arthur F. Schlesinger, Jr., *A Thousand Days: John F. Kennedy in the White House* (Boston, Mass.: Houghton-Mifflin, 1965), pp. 769–70.

2. More detailed treatment is provided in Howard J. Wiarda, *The Continuing Struggle for Democracy in Latin America* (Boulder, Colo.: Westview Press, 1980); *Politics and Social Change in Latin America* (Amherst: University of Massachusetts Press, 1982); and *Latin American Politics and Development* (Boston, Mass.: Houghton-Mifflin, 1979), with Harvey F. Kline.

3. Two classic studies are William F. Stokes, "Violence as a Power Factor in Latin American Politics," *Western Political Quarterly*, vol. 5 (September 1952), pp. 445–68; and Merle Kling, "Violence and Politics in Latin America," in Paul Halmos, ed., *The Sociological Review*, no. 11 (Keele, England: University of Keele, 1967), pp. 119–32. See also Howard J. Wiarda, *Critical Elections and Critical Coups: State, Society and the Military in the Processes of Latin American Development* (Athens: Center for International Studies, Ohio University, 1979).

4. For elaboration see Howard J. Wiarda, "Democracy and Human Rights in Latin America: Toward a New Conceptualization," *Orbis*, vol. 22 (Spring 1978), pp. 137–60; also *Human Rights and U.S. Human Rights Policy* (Washington, D.C.: American Enterprise Institute, 1982).

5. See Kenneth Karst and Keith S. Rosenn, *Law and Development in Latin America* (Berkeley: University of California Press, 1975).

6. The categories and the analysis that follow are derived in large part from a paper written by Margaret Daly Hayes, "Coping with Problems That Have No Solution: Political Change in El Salvador and Guatemala," in Alan Adelman and Reid Reading, eds., *Stability/Instability in the Caribbean Basin* (Pittsburgh, Pa.: University of Pittsburgh Press, forthcoming). The present statement only briefly summarizes her more detailed and penetrating analysis. The conclusions reached, however, are my own and not those of Dr. Hayes.

7. See the perceptive analysis of Jeane J. Kirkpatrick, "The Hobbes Problem: Order, Authority, and Legitimacy in Central America," in *AEI Public Policy Papers* (Washington, D.C.: American Enterprise Institute, 1981), pp. 127–37.

8. An attempt to set forth the parameters of what I have termed a "prudence model" of U.S. Latin American policy is set forth in two recent papers: "The United States and Latin America: Change and Continuity," in Adelman and Reading, *Stability/Instability in the Caribbean Basin* (chapter 3 in this book); and "Conceptual and Political Dimensions of the Crisis in U.S.–Latin American Relations: Toward a New Policy Formulation," in *The Crisis in Latin America* (Washington, D.C.: American Enterprise Institute, 1984).

6
Changing Realities and U.S. Policy in the Caribbean Basin: An Overview

Among the more serious handicaps faced by the United States and its Western allies in fashioning coherent, rational, consistent, and publicly acceptable foreign policy strategies is that their peoples—including many journalists, politicians, and even policy makers themselves, as well as the general population—often have only the most rudimentary and superficial knowledge of the foreign areas with which they must deal. The lack of sound knowledge, empathy, and deep understanding of cultures other than its own was a crucial problem—perhaps *the* most critical one—for the United States in Indochina and has been a serious handicap in Africa, Iran, and the Middle East. Because it is a contiguous and a "Western" area, we often assume we know Central America and the circum-Caribbean better than we know more distant areas; but it may be submitted that the same lack of empathy and understanding that afflicted policies in these other areas also plagues us in dealing with those now-turbulent societies on what we sometimes refer to as our "third border."[1]

America "rediscovered" Central America in 1979–1980 when the Nicaraguan Revolution led by the Sandinistas succeeded in overthrowing the Somoza regime, when Grenada also came under a leftist government and allied itself with Cuba, and when the four churchwomen were brutally massacred in El Salvador. The previous U.S. "discovery" of the circum-Caribbean had occurred precisely twenty years earlier with the coming to power of Fidel Castro and the establishment of a Marxist-Leninist regime in neighboring Cuba and led to a more-or-less sustained interest in the area through the mid-1960s. Both the earlier and the more recent "discoveries" of the region

Prepared for the Atlantic Council's Project on Western Interests and U.S. Policy Options in the Caribbean Basin, Spring 1983; to be published in a volume forthcoming from the council.

spawned a rash of "instant experts" and "instant analyses" that were far too frequently superficial, uninformed, and ethnocentric. The analyses we receive in the media and elsewhere almost make it seem as though Central American history began in 1979, that these countries had no previous background, sociology, or politics. The policies that have flowed from such analyses have often been similarly ad hoc and ahistorical.

This study seeks to help fill some of these gaps in our knowledge and understanding by furnishing useful background information, asking the kinds of questions that need to be asked, and providing the forms of interpretation that need to be employed. For the problems underlying policy for the United States and the Western allies in Central America and the circum-Caribbean are not just factual but conceptual. They have to do at least as much with the models of interpretation that we use to understand that area as with incomplete factual knowledge. Failure to come to grips adequately with both the factual situations prevailing in the Caribbean Basin and the mode and methods we use to analyze and comprehend the area is a prescription for far worse problems in the future.[2]

The Dynamics of a Changing Circum-Caribbean

The circum-Caribbean region, for the purposes of this study, includes Mexico, the states of Central America, Colombia, Venezuela, Guyana, Suriname, and the islands of the Caribbean. The region includes twenty-five independent states and sixteen dependent territories. There are current and former British and Dutch territories, units that are administratively a part of France, former Danish and Spanish colonies, and one U.S. commonwealth (Puerto Rico). The basin includes ten mainland countries and fifteen insular countries. It encompasses four larger and emerging middle-range powers (Colombia, Cuba, Mexico, Venezuela), thirteen smaller countries or what some have termed "city-states" (Jamaica, the Dominican Republic, Haiti, Guyana, Suriname, Belize, Guatemala, Trinidad and Tobago, El Salvador, Honduras, Nicaragua, Costa Rica, Panama), and eight what we might refer to as "mini-states."

The racial, linguistic, and ethnic background of the area is similarly diverse and complex. Eleven of the countries are Spanish-speaking. These countries have the largest populations by far, the most territory, the most resources. It is their histories primarily that we usually think of when we think about the area. But the Hispanic countries have recently been joined by nine English-speaking former British colonies; and the relations between these two groups of countries, in the Organization of American States and other international forums, are not always entirely harmonious. Their politics and sociologies are dissimilar as well.

In the island and mainland Hispanic countries, Catholicism is the dominant religion and Spanish the official or prevailing language; the culture, including society and the political culture, is strongly shaped by the traditions, customs, and institutions inherited from Spain. The religious and cultural situations—and the institutional arrangements—are quite different in the British Caribbean, to say nothing of the French, Danish, and Dutch areas.

In the mainland countries the major racial strains are Indian and European—though along the Caribbean rim of Central America, the so-called Miskito Coast (named for the indigenous Indians that inhabit this area, not for its stinging insects)—there are sizable minorities of Protestant, English-speaking blacks. Even the Indian-European mix varies greatly, however, between the heavy Indian concentrations of southern Mexico and highland Guatemala and the sparse Indian populations of Costa Rica and Panama. All the countries of this area are predominantly mestizo, but the size of their Indian subclass varies enormously. So does the degree of European (primarily Spanish) influence, and the mestizo majorities are made up of varying kinds of Indian-European mixes.

In the islands, the predominant racial strains are European and black, as contrasted with the European-Indian mix on the mainland. That is because the indigenous Indians on the islands were all but eliminated by the end of the sixteenth century, as much because of the diseases the colonizers carried for which the Indians had no immunity as because of force of arms or slave labor. As the Indians died off, Africans were brought in to replace them as manual laborers. Hence the societies and future histories of the islands would be described and written largely in terms of the interrelations between black and white, not Indian and white as in Central America.

But here again, variety abounds. In Cuba and Puerto Rico, the European population is larger, blacks are a minority, and the sizable mulatto element is quite light—"swarthy" as the racial slur of a past generation put it. Haiti, in contrast, is 90–95 percent black, but its chief institutions—government, land, money—were historically dominated by a small mulatto elite. In the next-door Dominican Republic, the white Hispanic elite is small numerically but very influential politically and economically, while the vast majority of the population, about 70 percent, is mulatto in varying degrees. Some Dominicans take pride in emphasizing that theirs is the only predominantly mulatto nation in the world; others would prefer to emphasize the country's Hispanic roots. Jamaica and the other former British colonies also have mulatto elites, a predominantly black mass, and often a small "Creole," or white, element—no longer enjoying political power except sporadically but still often influential financially.

There are small pockets of other ethnic-linguistic-racial groups, including Chinese, Japanese, Lebanese, Syrians, Jews, East Europeans, Italians, East Indians, Americans. These groups often have wealth and influence disproportionate to their numbers. With all these diverse ethnic and racial groups, it should be emphasized that the entire circum-Caribbean, in contrast to the United States, has until recently been quite free of intense racial hatred, conflict, and violence. The level of racial tension is increasing, however, fueled by the prevailing economic difficulties of the area, and in recent years there have been more race-related incidents and some outright racial clashes.

All the countries of the area are poor, but within that category there is, again, enormous variation. Barbados and Trinidad and Tobago have per capita incomes over $3,000 per year, which puts them roughly in the same category as the poorer European countries, Portugal and the Soviet Union. Mexico's per capita income is over $2,000 per year, similar to Brazil and Argentina; Mexico was long considered among the most successful of the newly industrializing countries, or NICs, but now that image is somewhat tarnished. Costa Rica and Panama, in the $1,700 range, are nearly twice as well off as Guatemala, Jamaica, and the Dominican Republic, and more than twice as well off as Honduras and Nicaragua. Haiti, with a per capita income of $270, the lowest in the region, is almost a hopeless case which, some feel, may collapse one of these years, calling for massive interventionist relief on someone's part, most likely the OAS or the United States. Basic data on all the countries of the region are provided in table 6–1.

As with income, so with various indicators of social and political modernity. Haiti is marked by the absence of viable institutional structures. Cuba is a Marxist-Leninist regime led by a charismatic caudillo. El Salvador, Honduras, Nicaragua (now dominated by the Sandinistas), and Guatemala have few stable, well-established institutions, while Costa Rica, Mexico, and Panama have a sizable middle class and some viable political institutions, albeit quite different in the three countries, that may see them through their present crises. The Dominican Republic has begun to develop democratic institutions, and Puerto Rico's present commonwealth status represents yet another special case. In general, the former Spanish colonies of the mainland and the islands continue to struggle with an older Hispanic legacy of authoritarianism, hierarchy, and patrimonialism; in contrast, the former British colonies of the Caribbean Basin retain the democratic institutions that are frequently referred to as the "Westminster model" and are among the few democratic nations left in the third world.[3]

All the countries of the area, however, are facing severe economic problems that are increasingly being translated into social and political strains. The worldwide economic depression has hurt them badly, markets for their main primary products are drying up, and the twin oil shocks of the 1970s have devastated them. With the exception of Mexico and Venezuela, these are all energy-deficient nations that must rely heavily on oil imports, and the sad fact for them is that it now takes two, three, four, or more times as much sugar, coffee, or bananas to buy a barrel of oil as it did only a few years ago.

Economic depression and stagnation, or in some cases even contraction, are now being reflected in rising social tensions and political conflict—Central America, the Dominican Republic, Jamaica, Guyana, Suriname, even Colombia, Mexico, and Venezuela. The economic downturn has occurred at a time of accelerated social change and of heightened expectations for a better life that the governments of the area are unable to provide. In part because of this, the increased social and political pluralism that one finds throughout the area has not produced very many happy, liberal, democratic regimes. Rather, particularly in the Hispanic countries but also in Grenada and Suriname, it has tended to provoke fragmentation, polarization, conflict, and breakdown. Indeed at the base of the political crises now destabilizing much of the region is a profound economic crisis that holds the possibility of undermining many of the democratic and developmental gains made in the Caribbean Basin in the last thirty years.[4]

Although it is not a sovereign nation, Puerto Rico merits attention in this regard. Puerto Rico enjoys, through its commonwealth status, a "special relationship" with the United States. Yet as neither a U.S. state nor an independent republic, Puerto Rico exists in a certain kind of limbo that many Puerto Ricans find no longer tolerable. Puerto Rico, moreover, has been affected by the same economic downturn plaguing other nations of the area, and it is increasingly being caught up in the political hurricanes and crosswinds now sweeping across the Caribbean. Puerto Rico is not formally a part of our study, but its problems are in some ways comparable to those of other countries here considered, and its internal problems and tensions are certain to reverberate beyond its own shores.[5]

Diversity and Common Features within the Area. The Caribbean Basin nations that are our chief concern here are diverse and complex. We do neither the area nor our policy analyses a service by lumping

TABLE 6–1

COUNTRIES OF THE CIRCUM-CARIBBEAN REGION

Country	Size (sq. mile)	Population (1981) est.	Per Capita GNP 1980 (US $) est.	Literacy (1982) est. (%)
Antigua	108	76,000	1,000	80
The Bahamas	5,389	249,000	3,790	93
Barbados	166	256,000	3,040	97
Barbuda	63	1,200	1,000	80
Belize	8,867	146,000	790	80
Colombia	439,405	26,730,000	1,180	82
Costa Rica	19,647	2,271,000	1,730	90
Cuba	45,397	9,796,000	1,360	96
Dominica	305	79,000	620	80
Dominican Republic	18,811	5,762,000	1,160	68

El Salvador	8,260	4,958,000	750	63
Grenada	133	107,000	660	unknown
Guatemala	42,031	7,201,000	1,080	47
Guyana	82,978	795,000	690	86
Haiti	10,711	5,099,000	270	23
Honduras	43,266	3,838,000	560	58
Jamaica	4,470	2,198,000	1,040	86
Mexico	767,919	68,236,000	2,090	74
Nicaragua	49,759	2,480,000	740	58
Panama	28,745	1,940,000	1,730	82
St. Lucia	238	124,000	690	80
St. Vincent	150	116,000	380	95
Suriname	70,000	385,000	2,130	80
Trinidad & Tobago	1,864	1,250,000	3,960	92
Venezuela	352,150	14,313,000	3,370	86

SOURCES: John D. Cozean, *Latin America 1982* (Washington, D.C.: Stryker-Post Publications, Inc., 1982); Inter-American Development Bank, *Economic and Social Progress in Latin America 1982* (Washington, D.C.: Inter-American Development Bank, 1982); National Foreign Assessment Center, *The World Factbook 1981* (Washington, D.C., 1981); World Bank, *Annual Report 1982* (Washington, D.C.: World Bank, 1982); Hana Umlauf Lane, ed., *The World Almanac and Book of Facts, 1983* (New York: Newspaper Enterprise Association, Inc., 1983).

them all into one undifferentiated category. Each country requires separate analysis, separate understanding, and separate policy initiatives.

Nevertheless, there is also a logic behind our focusing on the region as a whole. All of these nations lie close to the United States, along what has sometimes been termed "our soft underbelly," and athwart major Western trade routes. All of them (with Cuba and perhaps Nicaragua the chief exceptions) are closely tied to U.S. and Western markets. All of them are diplomatically, politically, and strategically of importance to us and, to a considerable degree, dependent on us. And all of them are facing severe economic disruptions which are helping to produce wrenching political traumas that also affect U.S. foreign policy and produce strains in the Western alliance.

There are other reasons for our focusing on the region as a whole as well as on its individual members. As "transitional" nations, neither fully modern nor wholly traditional, all these Caribbean Basin countries face some parallel developmental problems. All lie within what the United States has traditionally considered its sphere of influence, *mare nostrum*. All fall within the same categories, "American republics" or "Western Hemisphere" divisions, of our major foreign policy-making agencies. They come under the rubric of the Caribbean Basin Initiative, to say nothing of the OAS and other regional bodies. They themselves, moreover, are increasingly cognizant of the fact that they share a common destiny, common difficulties, and a certain psychological as well as geographic *place*. With the major influx of Caribbean peoples to our shores, the region *as a whole* has had a major impact on U.S. domestic politics and policy.

Finally, this entire area has taken on a new strategic importance for the United States, particularly as political breakdown has occurred in a number of states of the area and regimes deemed hostile to the United States have come to power. The fear in the United States is strong that this area can no longer be considered "safe" for U.S. interests, that political instability in some countries of the Caribbean Basin threatens the whole area, and that such chronic instability and potentially widespread upheaval provide opportunities for American and Western adversaries. Since it is seen as a regional problem, the argument runs, there must be regional solutions; and it is up to the United States to provide them. Those reasons for focusing on the common features of the area as well as on its diversity are also important.

U.S. Interests and Role within the Area. From its beginning the United States has had an interest in the Caribbean Basin area; but it was only in the late nineteenth century that the United States acquired both important stakes in the region and the means to play a major role. That is, it was only in the last decades of the nineteenth century that the United States acquired the industrial and military might to make its presence felt throughout the region; and it was around the turn of the century, with the acquisition of the Panama Canal Zone, Puerto Rico, the Virgin Islands, and a protectorate over Cuba, that the United States obtained major, tangible bases, investments, and interests to protect.

The Caribbean Basin has frequently been viewed both as an extension of our earlier expansionist notions of Manifest Destiny and as an area where vital U.S. interests are affected. As we examine the various nineteenth- as well as the twentieth-century U.S. schemes to incorporate, absorb, or dominate all or parts of the region, it is clear that we have always had special concerns in the Caribbean Basin. These concerns stem not just from considerations of self-interest but also from a desire embedded genuinely and deeply in the U.S. psyche to bring the presumed benefits of our civilization—democracy, elections, capitalism, human rights—to our poor benighted brothers in the Caribbean. That attitude helps explain why in that part of the world particularly, Realpolitik has frequently been jumbled together with missionary-like political and economic evangelism; indeed in U.S. policy toward the area, self-interest and moralism have often been virtually inseparable.[6]

The major U.S. interests in the Caribbean Basin are strategic, political, and economic. That is, the United States is interested in keeping hostile powers out of the area, maintaining its own networks of outposts and bases throughout the region, maintaining stability in the countries of the area in ways that are amenable to U.S. interests, and maintaining access to the markets and raw materials of the area. The encouragement of democracy and social, economic, and civic progress have been viewed as part of this overall strategy, as well as ethical "goods" in their own right. These interests have remained more or less constant since the turn of the century.[7] The matter is discussed elsewhere in this book and requires no further discussion here.

There are a number of questions, however, regarding the U.S. role and interests in the Caribbean Basin, which grow out of the changed circumstances of the present that must be raised for further discussion:

1. To what extent, with the massive migration of Caribbean Basin peoples to the United States in recent years, has the United States

itself become a partly Caribbean nation, and what are the implications of this for policy?[8]

2. The United States would seem to be a declining presence throughout the area in the past decade, while the Latin American nations have become more assertive and independent.[9] To what extent do these changes affect the U.S. role and interests throughout the Caribbean Basin?

3. New interests and issues—human rights, migration, employment, basic human needs, trade, the drug traffic, debt reservicing— have recently come to the fore; to what extent have these affected or supplanted the basic historical interests noted above?

4. To what extent has the presence of other outside powers in the Caribbean—West Germany, Japan, France, Spain, Italy, the Soviet Union, Scandinavia—as well as the rising influence of middle-level powers within the hemisphere—Argentina, Brazil, Colombia, Cuba, Mexico, Venezuela—made U.S. policy in the region more complex and difficult to implement?

These issues are of major importance; they lie at the heart of the analyses elaborated in this study.

Some Major Themes of the Study. That the nations of the Caribbean Basin are facing severe economic and political problems, that the region is in considerable turmoil, and that this has major implications for U.S. and Western policy concerns cannot be doubted. Within this context, however, several themes require special emphasis since they run as currents throughout not only this chapter but also our entire study:

1. While there are certain common themes and problems in the Caribbean Basin, the area is also characterized by immense diversity. There are both similar problems and particular ones, unity as well as immense complexity in the region.

2. While a great deal of attention is given over to the theme of "crises" in the Caribbean, the themes of continuity and "normalcy" deserve at least equal emphasis for many countries. Thus, while four or five nations of the region are presently in turmoil, nineteen or twenty of them are not—or at least not yet. Nor is turmoil an unprecedented feature of the circum-Caribbean landscape. But the point is, there is as much stability and continuity in the region as there is upheaval.

3. While outside analysts may proffer solutions for the area, the peoples of the Caribbean Basin are increasingly looking toward indigenous solutions and lesser dependency on foreign forces. How can

one blend and reconcile indigenous wants with outside pressures; and can the Caribbean Basin nations find their own way out or perhaps blend these with imported solutions? Are there other hemispheric models (Brazil with its developmentalist military, Venezuelan democracy, Mexico's one-party system, Cuba's socialism) as well as that of the United States?

4. What policies are appropriate for the United States and the Western allies in these changed circumstances; do the older formulas still serve adequately as a basis for policy, or are the new realities of our own situation and that of the Caribbean Basin so changed that new formulations are required?

The Historical Development and Diversity of the Area

The Caribbean Basin has long been what we may call an "imperial frontier."[10] From the sixteenth through the eighteenth centuries the fortunes of the major European imperial powers—Spain, France, Holland, England—were also played out in the Caribbean. Every major war fought in Europe during this period had its reflection in the Caribbean Basin, as the great powers jockeyed for colonies and advantage in this strategic region. The rise and decline of Spain, the growth of Holland as a major trading nation, the emergence of France as the dominant power on the European continent, and then the emergence of Britain as a global power can all be traced in the Caribbean Basin as well as in Europe. These powers continued to vie for influence and new outposts even in the nineteenth century, after most of Latin America had achieved independence. Despite French efforts to absorb Mexico in the 1860s and Spain's efforts both to hold on to Cuba and Puerto Rico and to reabsorb the Dominican Republic (all of which proved short-lived), by this point Britain had emerged as the dominant imperial power in the Caribbean Basin. Britain in turn began to be supplanted by the United States in the late nineteenth century and on into the twentieth century as the United States extended its suzerainty over the area.

Those nations in the area that achieved independence from Spain and France (in the case of Haiti) in the early nineteenth century were scarcely more fortunate than those that remained under colonial rule. The internal politics of Haiti, the Dominican Republic, Mexico, and the city-states of Central America were all, from the 1820s to the 1870s, marked by chaos, divisiveness, tumult, and considerable retrogression socially and economically from what had existed under colonial rule. A number of Spain's recently independent colonies reverted to more primitive forms of barter and subsistence, there was no agreed-upon principle of legitimacy, and breakdown and decay rather than "development" were the general patterns.

By the 1870s and 1880s some order had been brought out of the prevailing chaos. The first generation of postindependence caudillos or men on horseback had passed from the scene, and some of the early political battles over federalism, church-state issues, and the like had been resolved. This was also a period of growing immigration, some (as yet) limited infrastructure growth (roads, ports, communications), growing foreign investment, and some rising exports of primary goods. Some political institutionalization (new government agencies, political parties, associations) also occurred, and in some countries a modicum of stability was established.

The period 1890–1930 was one of unprecedented development in the region. The population increased, further institutionalization of armies and bureaucracies occurred, investment flowed in, and the economies of the area "took off," largely on the basis of commercialization and the export of raw materials and primary goods to the industrializing world. Four major patterns may be observed:[11]

1. continued colonial rule in the British, French, and Dutch Caribbean, the stability of which helped stimulate investment and export-financed development

2. order-and-progress caudillos (Díaz in Mexico, Gómez in Venezuela, Heureaux in the Dominican Republic) who brought development under authoritarian auspices

3. oligarchic rule (Costa Rica, El Salvador, Honduras) that nevertheless brought stability and development

4. enforced modernization in the early twentieth century, under U.S. Army or Marine rule (Cuba, the Dominican Republic, Haiti, Nicaragua, Panama)

As growth went forward under each of these patterns, new social forces were eventually set loose: a business-commercial elite, a rising middle class, trade unions. Tensions resulting from these influences began to be felt in the 1920s, beneath the surface appearances of prosperity and development. With the world market crash of 1929–1930, the elite-dominated systems governing in the area also came under attack.

In the meantime a significant change, already hinted at, had occurred at the international level involving changed relations of dependency. In 1898 the United States had displaced Spain's power in the Caribbean; at about the same time, it came gradually to replace Britain as the dominant economic and military power as well. One can even trace the dates when the United States supplanted Britain as the dominant trading power in the region: 1880s in Cuba, 1890s in the Dominican Republic, 1900s in Nicaragua, 1910s and 1920s in Honduras and Guatemala. The flag, as we know, to say nothing of U.S. customs agents, chewing gum, and baseball, soon followed the dollar. By the time of World War I and on into the interwar period and beyond, although there was still some competition among the major powers, the relations of dependency of the major Caribbean Basin nations were with the United States and no longer with Spain, France, or England.[12]

The period following the world economic crash of the 1930s was politically tempestuous. In a number of societies (Cuba, Venezuela, Mexico) the middle sectors moved to replace the traditional elites and to consolidate their own positions; elsewhere (Panama, El Salvador, Colombia) they lived in competition and uneasy tension with them. There were new middle-sector caudillos in the persons of Somoza, Trujillo, Ubico, Hernández, Gómez, and Carías; in Cuba, Guatemala, Mexico, Venezuela, and Costa Rica there were new middle-class (and often populist-reformist middle-of-the-road) political parties. But in general one can say that out of the elite-dominated societies of the pre-1930 period came a new societal equilibrium that was either middle-class dominated or based on a condominium of elite, middle-sector, and (sometimes) emerging labor elements.

The United States had also been influential in pushing change during this period. The formation of marine-created constabularies in such countries as the Dominican Republic and Nicaragua not only served as the avenues of advancement for dictators like Trujillo and Somoza but also helped to centralize power, to deprive the earlier regional caudillos in these countries of their power base, and to accelerate the rise of the mestizo middle class. During World War II, U.S. hegemony in the region was further increased, and Germany and Britain ceased to be major influences. In the postwar period the United States helped enforce economic liberalization in the region, which also implied greater political liberalization. Often these changes (for example, the creation of centralized, "professionalized" armies as distinct from regional caudilloism) were viewed as alien to the Central American/Caribbean (at least in its Hispanic parts) ways of doing things; and many observers are not convinced that enforced liberalization of societies still cast in part in an authoritarian mold was an appropriate strategy. In fact, by *forcing* a premature transition to democracy in some countries in the post–World War II period, we may have set the stage for the instability that followed.[13]

By the late 1950s and on into the 1960s, new challenges had

begun to undermine this middle-sector-dominated equilibrium. The Cuban Revolution was a major catalyst. But throughout the region new cracks were beginning to appear. Rivalries between and among the various middle sectors were endemic. Organized labor and peasant movements rose up to challenge the prevailing systems. Cuba and Puerto Rico felt increasingly uncomfortable with their histories of frustrated nationalism. Decolonization in the British and Dutch territories set loose new forces and new uncertainties. Revolutionary movements, with Cuba as their model, often aided and abetted by outside interests, emerged to challenge the existing legitimacy. Societies began to fragment, and political systems had difficulty coping.

For a time the reckoning was put off, through the sheer inertia that governs in most political systems, by living off borrowed capital both economic and political, and by means of substantial U.S. props and assistance. By the late 1970s these mechanisms of postponement were no longer sufficient or, in the case of foreign assistance, they had largely dried up. In some countries (El Salvador) the accommodative model of the past gave way to increased repression and the sclerosis of political institutions. Almost everywhere, including in the more democratic countries (Costa Rica, Venezuela, Mexico), a certain ossification had set in, along with immense corruption and/or inefficiencies. The two oil shocks of the 1970s were disastrous, along with the world economic recession that began to deepen in 1979. Rising social tension, racial conflict, violence, civil war (in some countries) ensued.

Later in this chapter we will present a model of interpretation that shows how the stagnant or contracting (in some countries) economies of the nations of the region helped to produce rising political tension and breakdown. It is in this context of crisis and breakdown that the present project on the Caribbean Basin was undertaken.

Impediments to Development

The nations of the Caribbean have not been blessed with an abundance of natural resources. Oil in Mexico and Venezuela has proved to be a mixed blessing, although—paraphrasing Pearl Bailey—being oil rich is still better than being oil poor. There is bauxite in Jamaica and Hispaniola, an abundance of good land in Cuba, pockets of gold, silver, nickel, and other minerals elsewhere. But these are scarce riches, and in fact the entire area is poor in natural wealth. The area does not have the minerals—iron and coal—necessary for industrialization, nor are the small pockets of these that do exist present in juxtaposition, as they were in western Pennsylvania during the period of the early industrialization in the United States. As Fidel Castro said some ten years ago in a statement he would now prefer to forget, the countries of the Caribbean Basin are so poor that revolution in them may cause only the destruction of the limited wealth that does exist or produce only the redistribution of poverty.

Geography and nature have been equally unkind. Both the islands and the mainland have steep mountains and mountain ranges that impede development and retard national integration. The mainland countries tend to be divided into *patrias chicas* out of which unified nations are only with difficulty forged; the islands have rocky spinal outcroppings that often limit settlements to the coasts. Good agricultural land is in short supply, and most of it is not amenable to mechanized farming. Transportation and communications systems are often primitive, designed and built initially by the marines or by the large foreign companies for the export of primary products and not necessarily to serve the broader public purpose. And, as an old geographer put it referring to the fact that none of the river systems serve the major population or industrial areas, "the rivers all flow the wrong way."

With the obvious exceptions of Mexico, Colombia, and Venezuela—the bigger nations—none of the countries of the Caribbean Basin has large enough internal markets to be economically viable, except in a quite limited number of products. Unlike populous Brazil or Argentina, for example, most of these city- or mini-states do not have the potential *ever* to become developed or industrialized nations. Based on their internal market size, they cannot support large-scale industry or manufacturing. It is almost un-American to say so, but realistic thinking in the policy area forces us to come to grips with the fact that for the majority of the Caribbean Basin countries, there may be no developmental light at the end of the tunnel. A few will continue to do modestly well on the basis of tourism, primary goods export, and some manufacturing; but there are likely to be few developmental "miracle" countries and only a few modest success stories.

Nor did the Central American Common Market or the Caribbean Free Trade Association serve appreciably or over a sustained period to increase the size of potential markets.[14] The fact is, first, that the nations of the Caribbean Basin are competitors in the world market *with each other* for the sale of the same primary products, chiefly sugar, coffee, and bananas. Unlike the French and West German economies after World War II, the economies of the Central American countries do not complement one another. Such complementarity is fundamental in explaining the success of the European Common Market as compared with the limited accomplishments (trade at one point reached $7 billion) of the several Caribbean schemes.

Second, political differences between the countries of the area have kept the common markets from working. For example, El Salvador and Honduras have old and historical grudges, the Spanish- and French-speaking islands of the Caribbean were never enthusiastic about joining the English-speaking part, democratic Costa Rica could not get along with Somoza's Nicaragua, and Cuba was ostracized. Economists concerned with the area have consistently lamented these political conflicts, but it may be that in thinking over any common market possibilities we should deal with such political differences realistically rather than just as "problems to be overcome."

The small size of the mini- and city-states of the Caribbean Basin has retarded development in other ways. In an excellent series of articles, Roland Ebel has argued that social organization and politics in a city-state are qualitatively different from those in a larger nation-state.[15] In Central America politics tends to be highly personalistic; family, clan, and clique oriented; patrimonialist; and organic. Everyone who counts knows everyone else who counts or is interrelated. The institutions appropriate for a larger polity—political parties, mass communications, elaborate and efficient bureaucracies—are not always seen as necessary in the city-state. Institutionalization has hence been retarded, and the agencies and programs created by American assistance have not consistently functioned as intended.

These factors have combined to produce other impediments to development. There are widespread educational and managerial deficiencies throughout the area. Mass illiteracy is still widespread, malnutrition and ill health are endemic, there are critical shortages of technical and vocational schools, the universities of the region are ill equipped to provide the leadership elites for the future. Western scholarship and fellowship programs have fallen behind. The number of trained administrators, for either the private or the public sector, remains abysmally small—although it has risen significantly in the past twenty years in all countries of the region.

The social, economic, and income disparities throughout the area are dramatically visible and plain for all to see. But perspective is necessary, and the oversimplifications that find their way into our media accounts must be corrected. This is not an area, necessarily, of teeming masses and rich, landed oligarchs. The oligarchies of the Caribbean Basin are not nearly (except perhaps in oil-rich Mexico or Venezuela) so affluent as their American counterparts; in most countries their income and living standards are, rather, at the level of the American upper middle class. The poor are poor by any standards; they want to improve their standard of living but would generally rather be left alone by all potential proselytizers and are not necessarily clamoring for guerrilla action. The middle class, in virtually all countries of the area, has by now not only become sizable but has also wrested considerable power from the old elites and now dominates many key institutions: army, Church, political parties, labor unions, universities, bureaucracy. There are immense social gaps and maldistribution of income, but these must be comprehended in their complex and changing dimensions. Our understanding of the Caribbean Basin nations will not be enhanced if we continue to view them in simplistic, essentially pre-1930 terms.[16]

Six main economic trends in the area help explain the tension and crisis in which the Caribbean nations now find themselves. The first has to do with the long-term balance of international trade, and it is this: Since roughly the 1920s the gap between the price that these countries receive for the export of their primary goods and the price that they must pay to import manufactured goods has steadily widened, making them progressively worse off in comparison with the industrialized nations.[17] Some analyses even suggest that within a decade the United States may be importing *no* sugar from the Caribbean, with potentially devastating effects on economies like that of the Dominican Republic. Related is the fact that these countries have been subjected to such severe fluctuations of prices for their single crops (whether coffee, fruit, or sugar) that their economies have been like roller coasters, with their governments often falling along with the price drops. Second, since approximately the early 1960s, with the emergence of large numbers of newly independent states in Africa and Asia, the nations of the Caribbean Basin have been undercut by these other countries that now produce the same agricultural crops (for example, sugar from Mozambique or Indonesia) as they do but have labor costs that are even lower.

Third, there is a long-term agricultural crisis in the Caribbean Basin area relating not just to lower prices but also to the scarcity of arable land, depletion of soil resources, abandonment of the land, and overemphasis on manufacturing and industrialization often at the cost of agriculture. Fourth, consumer habits in the importing nations have changed dramatically. We now drink more noncoffee drinks than in the past, we have "lite" beer and diet drinks rather than sugared ones, and we use sugar substitutes in all manner of foods. As a nation we are consuming proportionately less of what the Caribbean produces than in the past. That change may be beneficial for our collective and individual figures and blood pressures, but it is disastrous for the Caribbean Basin economies whose production of these commodities is largely locked in and cannot be changed quickly.

Fifth and sixth are the catastrophic oil shocks of the 1970s and the severe depression, precipitating the current debt crisis, in which the nations of the Caribbean Basin have been locked since 1979.[18] The worldwide economic downturn of recent years has, if anything, had a more devastating effect on the economies of the Caribbean nations than it has on our own economy or on those of the other industrialized nations. Indeed, at the root of the political instability in Central America is a severe economic crisis, precipitated by both the longer- and the medium-term causes identified above. Let us turn to the implications of these economic problems for the social and political systems of the Caribbean nations.

Change and Breakdown in the Caribbean Basin

The argument that there is a logic and *system* of Latin American politics often comes as a shock to outside observers. The outsider's images of Latin America, largely shaped by television headlines and *New Yorker* cartoons, are of such constant revolutionary upheaval as to be comic-opera and devoid of all system.

In fact, the politics of the area is quite systematic, though less so in the underinstitutionalized countries of the Caribbean Basin than in the larger and more established polities of South America and Mexico. Moreover, the "system" that exists is quite different from our own. Let us briefly examine what that system is and how it works, as well as how the cumulative economic changes discussed above affect it.[19]

In nineteenth-century Latin American society the three main political actors were the Church, the army, and the large landowners. Power tended to be centralized, authoritarian, personalistic, patrimonialist, and vertical-corporate.

But toward the end of the nineteenth century and even more so in the twentieth, not only did the older historical groups such as the Church and the army begin to change, but also new groups began to demand admission to the system. These included the newer business-commercial elites, then the middle class, and eventually trade unions and peasants. Under the rules of the Latin American political game, in which both military and civilian movements could play a role, new groups could be admitted to the system,[20] but generally only under the auspices of the government or the other elites. The Latin American systems gradually became more pluralistic, but this was usually a controlled, regulated, and limited form of pluralism, not the unfettered hurly-burly of American interest group pluralism. It is to be emphasized, moreover, that change could come through either electoral or nonelectoral means—that is, through civilian or military direction. In these ways the Latin American systems could both respond and accommodate to change, albeit in a limited way, without the traditional wielders of power being destroyed in the process.

Two conditions were necessary for the admission of a new group or "power contender" into the system:[21]

1. It had to show that it was strong enough numerically, politically, or financially to challenge the system sufficiently that its voice *had* to be heard in national councils. In this fashion the business-commercial elites came to be absorbed into the system by the time of World War I, the middle class was accommodated beginning in the 1930s, and organized labor began to make its voice heard from approximately the 1950s on.

2. The group had to agree to abide by certain commonly held and culturally approved understandings. It was not permitted to destroy other groups in the system by revolutionary means. And each group had to agree to accept, more or less, its place in the system and could not put forward exorbitant demands on which it would not compromise.

This system, implying evolutionary change and the gradual absorption of new groups into the political process without the old ones being destroyed or the basic structure of society being upset, worked tolerably well from roughly the turn of the century to the 1960s. Since then, however, the system has become more and more prone to breakdown. The question is, why? What factors have accounted for the fragmentation and polarization that we see all around the Caribbean Basin? Answers to these questions go a long way toward explaining the present crisis in the region and the dilemmas of American foreign policy toward it.

The fragmenting and polarizing factors to be emphasized here are long term and fundamental, as follows:

1. *Failures of political power sharing.* In Nicaragua the Somozas refused to share access to power and its spoils with anyone beside their own retinue; in Guatemala the normal course of sociopolitical development was perverted after the counterrevolution of 1954; in El Salvador the coup of 1972 denied the strategy of gradual accommodation to new groups that had been followed in the 1950s and 1960s. It is worth noting that in all these cases it was democracy in the Latin American sense (accommodation and "power-sharing," as described in the model above) that was rudely violated, not necessarily or so importantly democracy (elections and party politics) as North Americans understand it.[22]

2. *Economic decline.* The accommodative model of Latin American politics described above is based on one big assumption: an ever-expanding economic pie. To add new groups to the system without sloughing off older ones requires more and more new pieces to hand out to these newer claimants. For a long time in the 1950s, 1960s, and on into the 1970s the Latin American economies did register impressive growth rates of 3–5 percent or more per year, but since then stagnation and even contraction have set in. One need not go beyond our own society to understand that a zero-sum or negative-sum "game" in the economic sphere soon gives rise to increasing political competition, tension, even violence. In the Caribbean Basin, where because of external dependencies the world depression has been even more severe than in the Western industrialized nations, not only are there fewer economic pieces to hand out but this contraction economically has undermined both the existing regimes-of-the-moment and also the whole accommodative system described above, provoking sharp, even revolutionary challenges to it.

3. *Mass challenges.* The accommodative model of change worked best in a pre-1960s context where it was the business elites and the middle sectors that needed to be absorbed. These groups shared certain assumptions—that is, a "gentlemen's" understanding of accepted, permissible behavior. But the newer groups that have risen to prominence since then—organized labor, leftist parties, peasant and guerrilla elements—do not always share these same understandings, are organized on a different basis of legitimacy, and often explicitly reject the earlier rules of the game. The accommodative model by which Latin America *historically* adapted to change has proved far more viable and functional in absorbing rising business and middle-sector elites than in handling the rising mass challenges of the past two decades.

4. *The United States as a destabilizing force.* Two factors here command our attention. First, through our Peace Corps, AID programs, and other stepped-up developmentalist activities in the Caribbean Basin in the 1960s, the United States helped raise popular expectations in the area far beyond the capacity of the institutions there to cope with them. Second, when we did turn our attention to institutions, we tended to emphasize those institutions (elections, political parties, apolitical trade unions, and armed forces) reflective of the U.S. polity and not necessarily functional or realistic in the Caribbean Basin context. And in the process of imposing our own institutional preferences on the area, we tended to undermine those established institutions that were functional in that context or that might have presided over some difficult transitions. As a result, we have helped

produce in some Caribbean Basin countries the worst of all possible situations: rising, even revolutionary expectations, coupled with the absence of any viable institutional framework, either traditional or modernizing, through which these countries might cope with the pressures now thrust upon them.[23]

5. *Internationalization of the crisis.* The United States is not the only outside influence in the Caribbean Basin although because of its might and power and historic role in the region, it receives the most attention. The Soviet Union, Cuba, Argentina, Mexico, Venezuela, West Germany, France, and a number of West European political parties, trade unions, and foundations have also entered the arena. There are also transnational church and other groups. Not only does this situation make policy making more complex, but also it serves further to break down the isolation of the area, to introduce some new destabilizing influences, to involve the area in cold war struggles over which it has no control (and which frequently are of only peripheral interest or importance to the Caribbean Basin nations), and to prevent the possibility that the countries of the area could develop autonomously, without outside interference.

These factors help explain not only the recent instability in some Caribbean Basin nations but also the profound *systemic* crisis that they are now experiencing. The point needs to be stressed. What we are facing in the Caribbean Basin area is not just another round of the coups and revolts seemingly endemic to the region. Rather we are facing a crisis of a deeper and more profound sort that calls into question the entire developmental model on which these countries have been based since time immemorial as well as the bases of the strategies on which U.S. assistance and foreign policy have been grounded. Because the crises in the area are so deep and so pervasive, they will not be solved by simple formulas or easy palliatives. The situation today is in many ways comparable to that of the early 1930s when Latin America faced a similarly deep socioeconomic and political crisis, producing widespread instability and necessitating a fundamental reordering.

The *systemic crisis* described here helps explain the increased political tension and violence in the Caribbean Basin area and especially in Central America, the fragmentation and polarization, and the tendency toward breakdown, guerrilla movements, and civil war. That same systemic crisis helps explain the renewed search for self-identity throughout the region (including Puerto Rico) and the effort to find new or altered models of development. It also provides ample opportunity for meddling by a number of outside actors.

Political Interaction among the Caribbean States

Traditionally, the Caribbean Basin nations have existed in a kind of "splendid isolation," cut off not only from the rest of the world but also from each other. Cuba, Mexico, Puerto Rico, and the Dominican Republic had long been enveloped within the U.S. orbit, and other nations of the area have experienced occupations or been tied to the United States to a greater or lesser extent; but in the main the connections have, until recently, been minimal with the outside world and almost nonexistent with each other. There was little trade or contact among the Caribbean Basin nations, little in the way of political or diplomatic relations (except for some spectacular invasions and counterinvasions in the 1950s and early 1960s when tensions began to build, the so-called Caribbean Legion launched some armed efforts in the name of democracy to overthrow existing dictatorships, and Cuba made various efforts to export its revolution), and little interest or involvement in each other's affairs.[24] The lack of contact among the Caribbean Basin states was exemplified by the fact that telephone calls between the islands had to be routed through a New York exchange; air flights followed a similarly indirect route, with Miami or New York as the major transfer point. Between the islands and the mainland of Central America there was almost no contact whatsoever. All this has very recently begun to change, with major implications for the politics and international position of the area.

Modern communications and transportation have served to break down the traditional isolation of the Caribbean Basin. The changes wrought have been sufficiently treated and need no major elaboration. Radio, television, modern roads, the jet plane have not only brought new ideas, ideologies, and projects (to say nothing of tourists) to previously isolated areas, but also they have served to bind the Caribbean Basin together in new ways and to reemphasize the interdependence of the Caribbean states with each other and with the outside world.

The Cuban Revolution served as a powerful impetus to these changes. Cuba provided assistance to guerrilla movements in Venezuela, Guatemala, and the Dominican Republic during an earlier era, and more recently in Nicaragua and El Salvador; moreover, it also expanded the range of developmental options available and made the issues starker and more entangled. Instead of the older, two-part struggle of the 1950s and earlier between the democratic reformers and the conservative defenders of the status quo, both civilian and military, a third possibility was now added: a revolutionary dictatorship that broke with the United States and allied itself with the Soviet

Union. The Cuban Revolution complicated not only U.S. policy in the region but also, by providing another and radical developmental option, the domestic politics of every Caribbean Basin state.[25]

In response primarily to the Cuban challenge, the United States moved to strengthen its already existing military alliance system in the area and to promote regional economic integration. New military assistance pacts were signed with the major states of the area, and U.S. military aid was greatly stepped up. These efforts served to bind the Caribbean Basin militaries to the United States—through training programs, arms transfers, provision of military parts—in ways that were not so extensive before. But in recent years military assistance has been lowered, the military missions (except in crisis cases like El Salvador and Honduras) have been reduced, U.S. military influence has diminished, the military establishments of the area have begun to "shop around" for arms and equipment, and they have sought to diversify somewhat their international ties rather than rely exclusively on the United States.

The revolutionary upheavals, the rivalries, a declining U.S. presence, increasing arms purchases, and a struggle for control and dominance have also led to increasing conflict *within* the region and *between* its member states, often quite independent of U.S. strategies and initiatives. The Honduras–El Salvador "Soccer War" of the late 1960s, the Guyana–Venezuela border controversy, the conflict between Guatemala and Belize, the potential for conflict along the Mexico–Guatemala border—to say nothing of El Salvador's civil strife and the outside forces there, Cuba's involvement in various states of the area, and the conflicts along the Honduras–Nicaragua and Costa Rica–Nicaragua borders—suggest a strong possibility of even greater interstate turmoil and tension within the region than now exists. Potentially, these conflicts could ignite a regionwide series of conflagrations and end the historic peace that, in contrast with other geographic areas, has long kept Latin America free of major international wars.[26]

The common markets of the area, the Central American Common Market and the Caribbean Free Trade Association, have similarly fallen on hard times. The problems are, as we have seen, political as well as economic. The fact that these are competitive rather than complementary economies is not the "stuff" of which successful common markets are made. Political differences among the member states have also kept them apart. Some tariff barriers have been lowered, and trade in some products has increased; but the notion that these ties would also help lead to greater political and security interdependence among the Caribbean states has not worked out—except in limited ways and perhaps perversely in the sense of increasing the possibility that chaos and disintegration in one nation may foster the same conditions in its neighbors.

In addition, the fact that there is no visionary Alliance for Progress anymore and that U.S. assistance to the area is greatly down has further served both to retard economic development in the area and to give the United States fewer levers that it can wield. The diminished U.S. presence throughout the region—except in dramatic cases such as El Salvador and the Honduras–Nicaragua situation—has encouraged other outside actors to enter the Caribbean Basin while also providing possibilities for the Caribbean Basin nations to diversify their trade and international connections. I shall speak to these themes in more detail later in the discussion.

The decreased presence of the United States, to say nothing of the rising sense of crisis—even panic—in some countries of the area, has increased the interconnections among the Caribbean states in ways in which the earlier Alliance for Progress or the common markets did not. There are now non-U.S.-sponsored trade missions traveling between the several nations of the region and a variety of high-level diplomatic meetings dealing with such common problems as external debt, instability, political upheaval, and the possibilities for negotiation over Central America. Interestingly, as many of these meetings still occur in Washington—in the think tanks and other research centers—as they do in the Caribbean capitals themselves. Perhaps this is an indication that less has changed than is often thought; it also signifies the continued influence and leverage of the United States throughout the area, despite some loss of hegemony.

With a certain lessened presence of the United States (though the degree thereof and the question of whether the trend is reversible remain topics of hot controversy) and as a reflection also of the new assertiveness, self-confidence, and independence of many of the Latin American states, a number of new regional or "middle-level" powers and power centers have emerged in the Caribbean Basin. These include Cuba, Mexico, Venezuela, and Colombia. For the English-speaking Caribbean it might include Jamaica as well; for the smaller islands, Trinidad and Tobago is often a focal point. The presence of these new middle-level powers and the more active role they are playing (for example, Mexico's and Venezuela's oil initiatives and their efforts toward resolving the Central American conflicts) add a complex dimension not present in the Caribbean Basin before. For the United States and the Western allies, this greater complexity provides both problems and opportunities.

These and other changes discussed above have led the Caribbean Basin nations to begin to reassess their attitudes toward the United

States. Many see the United States as a declining power in the world and in the region. They reason that it is prudent, therefore, for them to reassess their historical ties to the United States and to begin to diversify their trade and their political and diplomatic relations rather than to rely exclusively, or nearly so, on the United States. The thrust toward greater independence from the United States is reflected not only in Cuba's, Nicaragua's, and Grenada's relations with the Soviet Union but also in the application of such countries as Venezuela, Colombia, and Costa Rica for admission to the nonaligned bloc.

Most pragmatic Caribbean Basin leaders (including some in Cuba and Nicaragua), however, recognize realistically the proximity of the United States, its power (albeit somewhat fettered), as well as their dependence on the United States, particularly economically. The United States is so big and the importance of its markets, capital, and technology such that realistic Caribbean statesmen recognize that they cannot escape from the American orbit, whether they wish to or not. As pragmatists, therefore, with the rhetorical flourishes concerning "dependency," "independence," and "third worldism" stripped away, their questions become: (1) How can we retain access to those all-important U.S. markets (including money markets) while also moving toward somewhat greater independence and diversity of relations; and (2) Given the still major U.S. influence, how can we channel U.S. programs and personnel into areas that help rather than harm, while also assuring that we and not the North Americans control our own developmental strategies?[27]

The pragmatic character of the majority of Caribbean Basin leaders and the way these questions of how to deal appropriately with the United States are raised make it clear that there is still ample room for U.S. and Western initiatives and policy in the area. These same questions, though, indicate as well how far our relations have come since the 1960s when U.S. influence was powerful and the United States was almost able to dictate both the foreign policies of the Caribbean Basin nations and much of their domestic policy as well. The situation now, in terms of trade relations, security concerns, our need for primary resources, political alliances, etc., is more accurately one of *interdependence* rather than the older situation of absolute Latin American dependence on the United States.

One final point meriting discussion in this section concerns the relations between the radical and the traditional states of the area and the question of whether "ideological pluralism" makes much difference. The answer is yes but with some qualification. Cuba, Grenada, Suriname, and Nicaragua, the radical states, have by now forged some close ties on a variety of fronts and with some common unifying ideological themes. These include suspicion of, fear of, and hostility toward the United States as well as hostility toward the "reactionary" regimes of the area and some assistance to those seeking to overthrow them. The radical states have also been clever in wooing the more moderate states, like Costa Rica, Jamaica for a time, and the Dominican Republic, with the goal of separating them somewhat from the United States. Thus far the more traditional states of the area have not been able to present a similar united front, and their diplomatic initiatives to rally greater international support (often led by the United States) have generally floundered.

Ideological pluralism in the Caribbean Basin, which has in some quarters become something of a code term for Marxist-Leninist regimes (while others think chiefly of left-socialist regimes like that of Jamaica's Michael Manley), therefore does make a difference. Potentially, it also calls into question a key argument often advanced in policy discussions: that the United States can live with "ideological pluralism" as long as that does not translate, à la Cuba, into an alliance with the Soviet Union. Now, obviously because there are different forms of ideological pluralism, it makes a major difference if one is speaking of the liberal and democratic socialism of Jorge Blanco in the Dominican Republic and Luis Alberto Monge of Costa Rica or the socialism of Fidel Castro or the Sandinistas in Nicaragua. It would be preferable if the ideological pluralism of Sandinismo did not imply an alliance with the Soviet Union, and surely the economic leverage we have over Nicaragua coupled with the apparent reluctance of the Soviet Union to assist the Nicaraguan Revolution on a massive scale as it has the Cuban Revolution is cause for some lingering optimism that Nicaragua will not become a Soviet satellite.

One cannot be sure, however, that the Sandinista leadership thinks in terms of such American-style pragmatism, nor should one forget the frustrated nationalism, the embittered history, and the intense desire for a "place in the sun" of such states as Cuba and Nicaragua. To the United States, policies toward Cuba or Nicaragua historically are only minor elements in a complex foreign policy that encompasses 150-odd nations. To the Cubans or Nicaraguans, in contrast, their relations with the United States are all-consuming; and small and often-U.S.-occupied countries like these have both long memories and ample reason to be sour toward the United States. One would hope, therefore, that ideological pluralism could be translated, if that is their preference, into *independent* socialist regimes in Cuba or Nicaragua, and in the abstract that seems possible. In the historical experience of this area, however, with often intense and bitter feelings toward the United States, in such small states with large inferiority complexes a genuinely independent Marxist-Leninist regime may not prove feasible.[28] Neither is it certain that the United States would allow it to happen. The point is controversial, but it deserves serious consideration and not the pat answers one usually hears. Ideological pluralism sounds appealing, but the concept should not be romanticized, nor should the difficulties of maintaining a genuinely *independent* socialism in a country like Nicaragua be underestimated.

The Impact of External Actors

In an earlier section we showed how modern communications and transportation have led to an erosion of the traditional isolation of the Caribbean Basin nations, to the increased presence of new actors both national and transnational, and hence to increased complexity in the international politics of the area. Let us review the lineup of these new actors as a way of providing background for the discussion.

The U.S. presence, though diminished from the 1960s, remains considerable. One must distinguish between those countries where the United States maintains "normal relations"—for example, the Dominican Republic—and those where its role is extraordinary—El Salvador, Honduras, increasingly Costa Rica and Guatemala. In the former countries the U.S. presence in terms of personnel, AID programs, military missions, etc., is considerably less than fifteen years ago; hence our leverage is also considerably diminished. In the latter countries recent political upheavals have led to a major renewed U.S. presence both military and civilian, to a considerable increase in the number of U.S. personnel and programs, and to a quite heavy-handed, almost proconsular role by U.S. ambassadors. Except in these "extraordinary" cases (which we must recognize, nonetheless, may be becoming more the rule than the exception), the U.S. position throughout the area—politically, economically, militarily, diplomatically, intellectually—is considerably reduced from what it was two decades ago.[29]

A number of the more ideological critics of U.S. foreign policy, unable or unwilling to recognize this declining U.S. presence throughout the area, have suggested that while the U.S. political and military presence may be down in some countries, that slack has been more than compensated for by the rising presence of U.S. multinational corporations (MNCs). At least in the Caribbean Basin area, that argument does not seem to be factual. The facts are these: In the past few years, even in such "success" countries as Mexico and Venezuela, U.S. private investment has plummeted dramatically;[30] one does not find the hotels of the area jammed as in the past with U.S. businessmen; it is firms and consortia from other countries—such as Japan, West Germany, France, Italy, and Spain—that are getting the contracts for the building of dams, highways, port facilities, and other construction projects; U.S. companies, rather than clamoring to exploit the area, must be induced with much persuasion to invest there and be provided with guarantees as in such major programs as the Caribbean Basin Initiative. Instead of eagerly jumping in, most MNCs have been very reluctant to get involved in the area. They ask: "Would you invest at present in El Salvador or Guatemala, or even Costa Rica, Jamaica, or the Dominican Republic?" and the question is difficult to answer affirmatively. The evidence, at least for the Caribbean, provides scant support for the idea that U.S.–based MNCs have simply replaced the U.S. government as the strong arms of our foreign policies. Indeed, the evidence suggests that U.S. firms have decreased their investments in Central America and the Caribbean recently, not increased them.

Into this partial vacuum has come a host of other actors. They are not all of one stripe, and their roles and interests differ. A brief explanation for each is useful.

The Japanese presence in the area is growing, mainly in trade and commercial areas. One reason Japanese businessmen have been so successful (along with several Western European consortia) is that they are willing to accept contract terms (joint ventures, 51 percent or higher ownership by local interests) that many U.S. firms have not been willing to accept.

Since the mid-1960s there has been a growing West German presence in the Caribbean Basin region, with both commercial and political ends in view.[31] France, England, Spain, Italy, and the Benelux and Scandinavian countries have all established a presence. The Spanish role is particularly interesting not just for historical reasons but also because Spain would like to couple its entry into the European Community with a kind of mini-Lomé or quasi-commonwealth arrangement vis-à-vis Latin America.[32] In the cases of the other European nations one finds a considerable mix of motives: commercial, diplomatic, political. With regard to the political motives, the feeling is strong that some European countries have pursued a vocal and often highly moralistic stance in Central America not only because they see the issues differently but also, in part, because they wish to divert attention from domestic politics, because they want to satisfy a left-wing constituency, and because there are no costs involved to them.

Of equal interest are the activities of a number of European political parties, labor unions, and foundations in the Caribbean Basin nations. Until recently, it was U.S. groups of this sort that enjoyed a near monopoly in the region. That is no longer so. Both Christian-Democratic and Socialist and Social-Democratic groups, chiefly from Germany but not exclusively so, and also the Socialist International, have begun to play a major role, providing training programs for young leaders, travel grants, and scholarships. What makes these activities especially interesting is that in many cases it is difficult if not impossible to separate the strategies and programs of these groups from those of their sponsoring governments.

We have already discussed the role of such regional actors as Cuba, Mexico, Venezuela, and Colombia. Mention must also be made of such other middle-level hemispheric powers as Argentina, Brazil, and Canada. Argentina's clandestine and semisurrogate role in Central America has come under strong attack in Buenos Aires. The United States would like Brazil to fill that role, but Brasilia is reluctant and wishes to pursue a more independent course, including new commercial relations with Cuba. Canada has growing interests in the Caribbean Basin; but so far it has not opted for full membership status in the OAS, and its desires to avoid entanglements in the current storms and controversies brewing throughout the area have so far overridden the pressures for deeper involvement.[33]

Other transnational agencies have also become more deeply involved in the Caribbean Basin. There are now so many that one cannot begin to do full justice to the subject matter, but a partial listing provides some indication of their range. On the business side there is the Council of the Americas and the Caribbean/Central American Action; on the labor side there is the American Institute for Free Labor Development of the AFL-CIO. Religious and human rights groups have been especially effective in influencing the congressional debate. Think tanks and university centers like the American Enterprise Institute, the School of Advanced International Studies, the Center for Strategic and International Studies, the Carnegie Endowment, the Institute for Policy Studies, the Heritage Foundation, and the Wilson Center have launched major Caribbean study groups and projects. There are numerous special interest groups, associations of military officers, lobbying agencies, and others who have plunged into the Caribbean maelstrom.[34]

In the debate and policy struggle over Central America the OAS has probably been underused, but that regional body may not be equipped to play a much larger role. The Inter-American Defense Board and related agencies have not been significantly involved. The banks and lending agencies (the World Bank, the International Monetary Fund, Inter-American Development Bank), however, have been heavily involved, and their role needs to be examined. Serious questions have been raised as to whether their lending policies, specifically the austerity measures exacted from democratic governments, are appropriate or if they may not prove to be self-defeating. Questions have also been raised concerning the lending practices of the private banks, particularly since in the present crisis it is not just the loans of the big banks that seem to be somewhat at risk but those of smaller regional and local banks as well. Also negotiations and policies within the EEC, the General Agreement on Tariffs and Trade, and the Lomé conventions affect the Caribbean Basin nations; but for the most part these have been overwhelmed by the more immediate and pressing military/strategic crises enveloping the area.

Nevertheless, it is no longer the Western and the hemispheric influences alone that are at work in the area. Twenty-five years ago those who raised the specter of Soviet military/political penetration in Latin America were soundly ridiculed, and in fact the notion of Stalinist legions expanding into the area seemed far-fetched. Today that specter, while it should not be exaggerated, should not be entirely ignored. The Soviet presence in Cuba, Nicaragua, Guyana, and Suriname is strong and increasing; moreover with the development of Caribbean air bases, port facilities, and a mobile marine amphibious and landing force the Soviets now have the strategic capabilities that were entirely lacking a quarter of a century back. In addition, their strategy has changed from one of almost blissful lack of interest in and ignorance of the area to a much more vigorous, sophisticated, and informed policy of, through Cuba largely, aiding guerrilla elements in their efforts to overthrow existing governments, and of assisting democratic governments to increase their independence from the United States. Thus far, Soviet activities in the Caribbean Basin have been generally limited and restrained, but neither the United States nor its Western allies can assume such will always be the case.[35]

There are other international currents coursing through the Caribbean that merit brief mention here. We have mentioned the impact of the cold war in the Caribbean Basin area, and former Secretary of State Alexander Haig once seemed to be arguing that the East-West struggle might be centered there. But there is also a North-South struggle in this area perhaps as important as the East-West one. Indeed, it may be worthwhile to suggest that the Caribbean Basin is one of those key world regions where the East-West conflict and the North-South division intersect, with all the potential for discord and contention those terms imply.[36]

Second and again partly obscured by the larger and more dramatic crisis in Central America, the Caribbean Basin nations have been caught up in the movement toward third worldism. Third worldism includes not just the political agenda (nonalignment) and economic agenda (redistribution of the world's resources) with which we are familiar but also incorporates important and far-reaching intellectual initiatives.[37] Among these initiatives are various efforts on the part of Caribbean Basin intellectuals and statesmen to divorce themselves from U.S. political and developmental models and to fashion indigenous models more attuned to their own history and traditions. This movement is only beginning in the Caribbean, and any realistic Caribbean politician knows he cannot remove himself or his nation entirely from the U.S. umbrella. But the significance and long-term consequences of these steps ought not to be ignored.

A third consideration involves the themes of dependence, interdependence, and the "diversification of dependence." Virtually all the Caribbean Basin nations are dependent on the United States economically, militarily, politically, culturally. Most recognize realistically that they cannot sever those ties. But in this era of scarce natural resources, commodities, and primary products, the Caribbean Basin nations see a means by which they can reduce some of their ties of dependency in favor of a more complex and favorable (to them) situation of interdependence vis-à-vis the United States. They would also like to "diversify their dependence" by expanding their trade and other relations with Japan, Western Europe, the Soviet Union and Eastern Europe, perhaps China, the Middle East, Africa, and even other Latin American nations. These steps need not be looked upon with hostility by the United States. They reflect, in fact, some quite prudent and realistic steps by the Caribbean Basin nations. Resistance to such initiatives on our part is not likely to be very useful and may be counterproductive. A sounder strategy might encompass adjustment, accommodation, and understanding on our part, combined with a sense of realism as to how far such steps can go in "our backyard" and with a clear idea too of how our own interests can at the same time be served.

The presence of all these new international actors in the Caribbean Basin, national and transnational, has added a complexity to the international politics of the area that did not exist before. Its epitaph has been written before, but with the existence of all these outside forces in the Caribbean and the inability of the United States effectively to remove them or keep them out (even if it wished to do so), perhaps the Monroe Doctrine, as some have argued, is now indeed, finally, dead. The Monroe Doctrine, it may be recalled, sought to keep out not only all outside forces but also all outside ideologies. Given the still immense power of the United States in this part of the world and its apparent continued willingness to employ its influence in countries like El Salvador and Nicaragua, it is hard to believe the

Monroe Doctrine is entirely moribund. But it certainly requires re-thinking and amendment if it is to survive at all, the first step of which surely requires a realistic assessment of the new international actors present in the Caribbean Basin.

Goals, Interests, and Perceptions of the Caribbean States

The goals, interests, and perceptions of the Caribbean Basin states in the present context may be summarized briefly since they are quite clear and unambiguous and a number of these have already been discussed. Our concern is not only to list these goals of the Caribbean nations but also to examine how and where they are in accord with or diverge from the goals and interests of the United States and the Western allies. The goals of the Caribbean nations are as follows:

1. *Regime viability.* Any regime in the Caribbean area must, in the present circumstances of international upheaval and internal challenges to established ways, pay attention first and foremost to its own survival. The stability of the government in power cannot be taken for granted, as observers from the outside and particularly Western aid administrators are prone to do. Hence the first-order concern, before any public policies can be carried out, must be for securing the government's own power base. That often involves relations with the military, patronage concerns, wholesale bureaucratic reshufflings that are often, if not incomprehensible, downright exasperating to foreign analysts. In short, private and partisan concerns must be taken care of before the public ones receive attention.

2. *Sovereignty and territorial integrity.* Ordinarily this factor would be at a lower priority, but in the present Caribbean Basin context of border disputes (Venezuela–Guyana), disputed claims to sovereignty (Belize), armed interventions (Honduras–Nicaragua and Costa Rica–Nicaragua), efforts at subversion of existing governments (El Salvador, Guatemala), and multiple outside interventions or the fears thereof, it must be listed at or near the top. These matters are often frustrating to foreign aid administrators, private economic interests, and lending agency representatives who would rather get on with what they see as the "normal" business of development; but they are crucial to the Caribbean Basin nations since they involve such fundamental issues as the very existence and integrity of the nation. Leaders in these nations cannot ignore these factors or their own tenure in office (another "first-order" priority) may be quite short.

3. *Economic development and social progress.* Next to maintaining sovereignty, territorial integrity, and its own survival, economic and so-

cial development must be among the highest policy priorities of any Caribbean Basin government. This priority, too, is not necessarily or always in accord with U.S. interests that tend to focus heavily on strategic considerations.

4. *Democracy and human rights.* The Caribbean Basin countries genuinely want to have democracy and human rights (as distinct from only paying lip service to these goals, as sometimes also occurs), and they wish to have these in accord with universal criteria and understandings of these terms. But some of their leaders also wish it to be understood that democracy does not always work well in their context, that sometimes in emergency situations democracy and human rights must be suspended. They further wish it were better understood in the United States and the West that democracy and human rights in their countries often imply different meanings, emphases, and institutional arrangements than in the United States and Western Europe. Again, there is considerable room for divergence from U.S. criteria.

5. *Trade, commerce, investments, markets.* In the international sphere, these may be the highest-order priority of the Caribbean Basin states. Access to U.S. markets, capital, and technology is essential for the very survival of these nations. These interests run up against the growing pressures of protectionism in the United States and also against a continuing preoccupation in the United States with grand political designs (the East-West struggle, for example), which most Caribbean leaders view as tangential to their main interests. Again, the theme of divergent interests and priorities is repeated.

6. *Security, stability, order.* Caribbean leaders see very clearly the need to resolve what Jeane Kirkpatrick once called "the Hobbes problem" in Central America: the need for order, authority, and legitimacy.[38] They are quite aware of the dangers of outside intervention, as well as of the wrenching, centrifugal forces within their own societies. They would much prefer, however, that, with the proper assistance, they be left to deal with these problems in their own way. Heavy-handed military intervention by outside nations, the subordination of local ways of doing things to some presumably grander design, or a foreign ambassador's exercise of essentially proconsular roles (thus at times supplanting their own president or prime minister) is not acceptable.

7. *A place in the sun.* These are small nations with long histories of frustration and a strong sense of inferiority. They wish to be treated not as "banana republics" but with some measure of dignity and respect. They wish to see their accomplishments, however modest,

recognized, and they insist that they know best how to solve their own problems.

8. *Independence.* The Caribbean Basin nations recognize their dependence on the United States, and most leaders of the region understand and have faced that fact realistically. By diversifying their trade and international connections, however, they seek not to break relations and contacts with the United States—an entirely unrealistic step—but to expand their opportunities and to reduce if only slightly or psychologically the uncomfortable reality that they are "sardines" that can at any time be gobbled up by the giant "shark" to the north.[39]

9. *Alternative routes to development.* The era when the United States could dictate the developmental model its neighbors must take, or when the U.S. political and economic system was *the* system to emulate or even inevitably to follow (as much of the development literature of the 1960s put it), is fading. Rather than importing U.S. institutions and models that are inappropriate in their own circumstances, Caribbean leaders are increasingly looking to indigenous institutions, as well as to other outside models, and seeking to fashion their own route to development, or they are seeking a more propitious blend between imported institutions and their own local practices. They expect some understanding of these efforts and empathy from the outside. Indeed the fashioning and institutionalization of such indigenous developmental models are likely to be the next great innovative steps, in the Caribbean as in other areas of the third world and in the social sciences.[40]

Goals and Interests of the Northern, Western, and Industrialized Countries—and of Regional and Global Institutions

Let us state these goals and interests in summary fashion since they are largely familiar to us. One of our key purposes is to see the degree to which these goals and interests of the Northern, Western, and industrialized countries are compatible among themselves and with those of the Caribbean Basin nations.

United States. U.S. goals and interests in the Caribbean historically may be summarized as follows:

1. *Security interests:* guarding of our "southern flank," securing access to sea lanes, maintaining bases and listening posts, preventing foreign powers from gaining a foothold, securing our borders

2. *Economic interests:* maintaining access to the markets, raw materials, labor supplies of the area

3. *Political interests:* maintaining stability in ways that are compatible with our interests, including allowing for change that is not radical or uncontrolled

4. *Economic development and social progress:* assisting modernization both as a good in itself and as a contribution to 1, 2, and 3 above

5. *Democracy and human rights:* emphasizing democratic development and human rights, but in times of crisis this interest is often subordinated to 1, 2, and 3 above

In considering U.S. goals, interests, and perceptions in the Caribbean Basin, several questions come to mind. The first has to do with the traditional sense of superiority, smugness, condescension, and lack of empathy and understanding toward the Caribbean nations and peoples that is so deeply ingrained in the U.S. psyche. In this era of rising Caribbean nationalism and independence, are such attitudes appropriate and functional; can they be changed?[41]

Second, what about Puerto Rico and the status question? Many analysts are concluding that Puerto Rico is a potential time bomb for the United States. What can and should be done with the Puerto Rican issue at this stage?

Third, as the United States itself has become something of a Caribbean country, what will be the impact of such a large number of Hispanic Americans and Caribbean Americans, with a rising political consciousness, on our policies toward their native countries? A series of related questions may be asked with regard to black Americans and their growing interest in Caribbean affairs. The case of Haiti and Haitian refugees comes quickly to mind.

Fourth, to what extent have the historical and traditional goals of U.S. policy in the Caribbean Basin as noted above been supplanted by new goals and interests: human rights, immigration issues, drug traffic, illegal aliens, debt questions, the potential for massive instabilities on our very doorsteps, basic human needs concerns, population policy, jobs and protectionism, foreign labor supplies, pressures on schools and social services? How do these new concerns affect American bedrock interests, are they compatible with them, what can give?

Fifth, given our own economic cutbacks, what can be expected in the way of new aid packages and military assistance programs? Surveys of public opinion (and, by reflection, of the U.S. Congress) indicate that there will be no large-scale assistance programs as in the 1960s;[42] if that is so, what levers does the United States have to help shape Caribbean developments?

Sixth, looking at the Central American imbroglio, as well as the domestic debate and media coverage of Central American events in recent years, many seasoned foreign policy observers have strong doubts that the United States can successfully carry out *any* serious, rational, sustained policy in the region. When that disability is combined with our economic difficulties, the lack of funds or public support to carry out any but the most modest of foreign aid programs, our inefficiencies and incapacities both civilian and military, our internal divisiveness, and our lack of will, serious questions must be asked concerning our capacity and ability to fashion and implement any major new Caribbean policy. Recognizing these constraints need not force us into what General Andrew Goodpaster neatly calls the "doctrine of preemptive concessions,"[43] but it does, one hopes, introduce some realism into the discussion.

Finally, we must ask how and where and to what degree U.S. goals, interests, and perceptions are compatible with those of the Caribbean Basin states. Several glaring contradictions, worthy of further discussion, are immediately apparent. First, U.S. attitudes of arrogance, haughtiness, condescension, and some contemptuousness are incompatible with the Caribbean desire for respect, dignity, a place in the sun, and freedom to pursue their own institutional and developmental models. Second, the U.S. emphasis on stability may not be compatible with the Caribbean desire for accelerated change. Third, we seem to be concentrating still on grand political, security, and strategic designs when the Caribbean desire is for trade, trade, trade. Fourth, our efforts to resurrect the much buffeted inter-American defense arrangements and our attempts again to envelop the Caribbean within our sphere of influence may be at cross-purposes with their own efforts to reduce their dependency and diversify their international connections. And fifth, while we continue to talk of U.S. policy *toward* the Caribbean Basin, of their dependence on us, the real situation at present seems to be a more complex one implying a greater *interdependence* than in the past. We are now almost as dependent on Latin America for our needs—oil, minerals, markets, foodstuffs, industrial goods, and, not least, allies—as it is upon us.[44]

These questions are difficult and serious; they force us to begin thinking about what kind of U.S. policies toward the Caribbean one can reasonably expect.

Western Europe, Canada, Japan. The increasing presence of the other Western, democratic, and industrialized countries in the Caribbean Basin area has already been discussed. For the most part their interests and those of the United States are compatible. That is, they also have an interest in stability and order, economic and social progress, regional security, democracy and human rights, trade, commerce, and investment.

But there are differences with the United States as well. First, it is probably fair to say that the interests of Western Europe, Canada, and Japan are concentrated heavily in the trade, commerce, and investment areas, and less so on the strategic and security issues. These different concerns have to do, obviously, with the fact that the Caribbean lies right on the southern border of the United States but is considerably distant from these other nations. Nonetheless, the concentration of the other Western, democratic, and industrialized nations in the trade and commercial area may be closer to what the Caribbean nations want than is the case of the United States.

Second, the foreign policy interests of the other Western democracies with regard to the Caribbean are in some areas at variance with those of the United States. In part this difference reflects genuinely different perceptions and readings of the situation in the area; in part it reflects an ethnocentrism on the part of these other Western countries that is at least as pronounced as that of the United States; in part it reflects a response on the part of these governments to domestic political pressures; and in part it reflects the luxury not available to the United States of being able to stake out bold initiatives in this foreign policy area without having to pay the price or endure the responsibilities of their pronouncements.

But there are also sufficiently strong common bonds and interests concerning the Caribbean between *all* the Western industrialized democracies that a more coherent and unified approach might be pursued. Nor should the growing presence of these countries in the Caribbean necessarily be viewed with suspicion and hostility by the United States. If the United States has itself been a declining presence throughout the area in the last fifteen years, one can think of far worse scenarios than to have West Germany, France, Spain, Japan, and some others fill part of the void. There is evidence that is already happening. A greater European, Japanese, and now Israeli presence will clearly make U.S. policy making with regard to the area more complicated, but there are useful or potentially useful aspects to these new relationships as well that seem worth exploring.

The Role of Regional and Global Institutions. The United States would generally prefer to work through regional institutions (such as the Organization of American States, the Inter-American Defense Board, the Pan American Health Organization, the Economic Commission for Latin America), which historically at least and to a considerable extent today it can control, than through global institutions such as the United Nations, where the United States is now a lonely minority. When there are disputes in the region, the first inclination of the United States is to act unilaterally; where such action is not feasible or where we have a desire to provide multilateral legitimacy to a unilateral action, the usual advice is to "go OAS." The United Nations, in contrast, is often viewed by the United States as an interloper in hemispheric affairs, although because of its third-world majorities, some Caribbean Basin states on some issues would clearly prefer to "go UN."[45]

The issue of regional versus global deliberative bodies as sounding boards and conflict solvers is complicated by several factors. The first is the split within the regional agencies, chiefly between the English- and Spanish-speaking countries. The dispute was apparent in the conflict between England and Argentina over the Falklands/Malvinas; it also surfaces in the desire of the small English-speaking countries of the Caribbean to have Canada assume full OAS membership, as a North American counterpoint to the United States and as a kind of "big brother" for the other English-speaking countries. As yet, the English-speaking countries within the OAS have not been fully integrated into the organization, which makes the effectiveness of that regional body less than what it might be.[46]

Second, there is the issue for the United States of a global versus a regional foreign policy, or a "special relationship" with Latin America. Historically there has always been a special relationship with Latin America for reasons of geography, religion, politics, culture, and a common New World past; but under President Carter that concept was abandoned in favor of a "global" policy and bilateral relations. Obviously there is room for both a global and a regional approach, depending on the issue and the context. A number of the larger countries of South America prefer, in at least some areas, bilateral relations with the United States. But among the smaller states of the Caribbean Basin, a regional forum is often preferred since in a bilateral negotiation with the United States they are woefully at a disadvantage. Clearly a balance between a global and a regional approach would be most useful, but at present that implies efforts to reforge the special relationship as well as a restrengthening of regional bodies like the OAS.

The North-South dialogue, third, also impinges on the regional/global issue. Since Cancún, there has been little forward motion of the North-South dialogue. In part this stalemate is due to U.S. reluctance to resume what is often regarded not as a dialogue but as a catalog of third-world demands. In part also, it has to do with discussions within the U.S. government as to where the dialogue should take place (GATT, the United Nations, the OAS, or some specialized agency), what issues should be discussed, how binding the decisions should be.[47]

For their part the states of the Caribbean Basin are not of one mind on these issues either. Naturally, and in the abstract, the Caribbean nations are sympathetic to third-world positions and could be expected to champion them. At the same time some Caribbean states such as Mexico, Cuba, or Venezuela think of themselves as *leaders* of the third world and not just one among many. The problem is further complicated by the situations of Cuba and Nicaragua who, if they were to be invited to some North-South forum, could be expected to use the opportunity to castigate the United States rather than to participate in much real dialogue. Finally, after all this, it must also be stated that most Caribbean Basin nations are rather tepid followers of third worldism because as pragmatists they recognize that ideological posturing goes only so far and that in the long run they must deal realistically with the United States.

Fourth, the debt question has posed a major if not *the* major concern of many Caribbean nations. They must rely on agencies like the World Bank, the IMF, and the IADB; but they would strongly like to give themselves a more powerful voice in the deliberations and policies of these bodies. And in both global and regional policy making, Caribbean nations feel their proximity to the United States should afford them special treatment by the lending agencies. The debt question is so crucial that it must now enter into any discussion of appropriate U.S. and Western policy toward the Caribbean Basin.

In all these areas—whether the question centers on the goals and interests of the Caribbean Basin nations, those of the United States and its Western allies, or the roles of the regional and global institutions—there are many areas of conflict, discord, and disagreement. But there are also, as made clear in the analysis, opportunities for discussion, dialogue, compromise, and accommodation. Moreover, given the difficulties of U.S. bilateral relations, there are now many voices arguing for a strengthening of the multilateral agencies. The present overview helps provide some guidelines for understanding the areas of conflict as well as suggesting where there is room for accommodation.

Groping toward Policy

Specific recommendations for U.S. policy are contained in the Policy Paper prepared by the Atlantic Council's Caribbean Basin Working

Group;[48] here let us only summarize the discussion and suggest some general guidelines for policy.

First, it is necessary to reemphasize the diversity, as well as the common problems, of the Caribbean Basin. For some purposes this area may be treated as a single unit, for others not. What works in some countries may not work in others. There are immense differences of history, culture, geography, language, politics, society, economics. Certain common themes and problems, with appropriate qualification and nuance, do apply to all or most countries of the area; but for policy to be effective, individual and country-specific programs must be fashioned. No one policy blanket will be appropriate for the entire area. The beginning of wisdom in a policy sense is to recognize both the common features and problems of the area and the intense individuality of each case.

Second, we must recognize the nature of the crisis in the Caribbean. It is long-term and systemic, not short-term and easily resolvable. No one U.S. administration can solve this longer-term crisis; a generation or more of a coherent, rational, sustained policy will be required. Easy palliatives and panaceas will not do; patience and persistence may. At the same time one should not overstate the severity of the crisis or assume that its effects are everywhere the same. Most countries in the area are doing reasonably well under the present circumstances; others are limping along but with few prospects of imminent breakdown. Only three or four countries of the area have reached an advanced state of disintegration, commanding dramatic headlines. The crises in these nations are troublesome obviously, but one should be careful neither to understate nor to overstate the severity of the Caribbean situation.

Third, we must come to grips with the new realities of the area. These have to do with the changed, considerably lessened, presence of the United States throughout the area and, at the same time, with the fact that we have become something of a Caribbean nation and, to some degree, ourselves dependent on that area. The new realities also include changes within the Caribbean Basin nations: their desire for greater independence, their desire to diversify their trade and international connections, the growing assertiveness of some of the nations of the area, their collective and individual desires for a place in the sun, their third worldism, their efforts to fashion indigenous institutions rather than slavishly imitating imported ones, the accelerated social changes and rising pressures within their own populations. The new realities include the presence of new outside actors in the area: the Soviet Union, Western Europe, Japan, the middle-level powers of the Western Hemisphere, a variety of private groups and agencies that may be termed transnationals.

All these "new realities" present both problems and opportunities for U.S. policy and that of the Western allies. They undoubtedly make the situation far more complex than was the case thirty years ago. They make it far more difficult for the United States to carry out policy. They raise the specter of failure as well as the possibilities for success.

A useful albeit simplistic caveat might be that when the United States is faced with new realities, it must reassess its policy realistically. Simply railing against these new realities and wishing they would go away will not suffice. U.S. policy and that of its Western allies must adjust to the new *facts* visible throughout the Caribbean Basin nations. We must adjust to our own, generally lessened presence and weaker position throughout the area. We must adjust to the new European presence and that of the other middle-level powers in the area, rather than viewing these consistently as threats. We must take account of the new Soviet presence in the area (and the Cuban one), which is no longer a phantom threat but a real one. Perhaps most important, we must adjust to the changed realities of the Caribbean Basin nations themselves and their growing assertiveness, independence, and desire for change.

In Chapter 8, I have suggested a "prudence model of U.S.-Latin American policy."[49] That stance implies neither benign neglect on the part of the United States in the Caribbean Basin nor what might be called heavy-handed proconsular interventionism. The prudence model is posited on realism rather than on romance and wishful thinking in our foreign policy assessments, on restraint and on the recognition of the limits to what the United States can and cannot accomplish in the area. It is based on greater empathy and understanding of the Caribbean Basin nations and on some unaccustomed deference and modesty on our part, but still on a leadership and catalytic role for the United States primarily in the economic sphere, on a renewed "special relationship" with Latin America, on political and strategic leadership that is restrained rather than arrogant and overbearing. These are all happy phrases that obviously need to be fleshed out and to come up against the hard realities of tough policy choices in individual cases. Such a "prudence model," however, may well serve as a starting point for the discussion.

Notes

1. Thomas P. Anderson, *Politics in Central America* (New York: Praeger, 1982), as well as the thoughtful review of that book by Don Oberdorfer in the *Washington Post*, June 27, 1982. My own analysis of these problems of empathy and understanding in dealing with Latin America is contained in Howard J. Wiarda, ed., *Politics and Social Change in Latin America: The Distinct Tradition*, 2d rev. ed. (Amherst: University of Massachusetts Press, 1982).

2. Some of the better studies include Richard Millett and Marvin Will, eds., *The Restless Caribbean: Changing Patterns of International Relations* (New York: Praeger, 1979); H. Michael Erisman and John D. Martz, eds., *Colossus Challenged: The Struggle for Caribbean Influence* (Boulder, Colo.: Westview Press, 1982); and Richard Feinberg, ed., *Central America: International Dimensions of the Crisis* (New York: Holmes and Meier, 1982). For a consideration of some of the conceptual problems in interpreting Central America, see Howard J. Wiarda, "The Central American Crisis: A Framework for Understanding," *AEI Foreign Policy and Defense Review*, vol. 4, no. 2 (1982), pp. 2–7, as well as Howard J. Wiarda, ed., *Rift and Revolution: The Central American Imbroglio* (Washington, D.C.: American Enterprise Institute, 1984).

3. Vaughn A. Lewis, "Political Change and Crisis in the English-Speaking Caribbean," Paper presented at the Conference on the Caribbean, University of Pittsburgh, October 1982; see also the forthcoming volume edited by Myron Weiner and Ergun Ozbudun, *Competitive Elections in Developing Countries*, especially the introduction by Weiner.

4. Gary Wynia, "The Economics of the Central American Crisis," in Howard J. Wiarda, ed., *Rift and Revolution*.

5. Puerto Rico has been the subject of a number of recent conferences and special reports by several Washington-based research centers, including the American Enterprise Institute, the Wilson Center, and the Carnegie Endowment.

6. See the two volumes of Lester Langley, *Struggle for the American Mediterranean, 1776–1904* and *The United States and the Caribbean in the Twentieth Century* (Athens: University of Georgia Press, 1976, 1980); see also Howard J. Wiarda, ed., *The Continuing Struggle for Democracy in Latin America* (Boulder, Colo.: Westview Press, 1980), especially the introduction entitled, "Is Latin America Democratic—And Does It Want to Be?"

7. Howard J. Wiarda, "The United States and Latin America: Change and Continuity," Paper presented at the Conference on the Caribbean, University of Pittsburgh, October 1982, in Alan Adelman and Reid Reading, eds., *Stability/Instability in the Caribbean* (Pittsburgh, Pa.: University of Pittsburgh Press, forthcoming); chapter 3 in this book.

8. Jorge I. Domínguez, *U.S. Interests and Policies in the Caribbean and Central America* (Washington, D.C.: American Enterprise Institute, 1982).

9. Luigi Einaudi, ed., *Beyond Cuba: Latin America Takes Charge of Its Future* (New York: Crane-Russak, 1973).

10. Eric Williams, *Capitalism and Slavery* (New York: Russell, 1961); Juan Bosch, *El Caribe: Frontera Imperial* (Madrid: Alfaguara, 1970).

11. The developmental patterns are traced in Howard J. Wiarda and Harvey F. Kline, eds., *Latin American Politics and Development* (Boston, Mass.: Houghton-Mifflin, 1979).

12. Howard J. Wiarda and Michael J. Kryzanek, *The Dominican Republic: A Caribbean Crucible* (Boulder, Colo.: Westview Press, 1982).

13. Wiarda, *The Continuing Struggle for Democracy;* and Michael Grow, *The Good Neighbor Policy and Authoritarianism in Paraguay: Economic Expansion and Great Power Rivalry in Latin America during World War II* (Lawrence: University of Kansas Press, 1981). A more general article on this theme is forthcoming by Grow and Wiarda.

14. For an overview, see Stuart I. Fagan, *Central American Economic Integration: The Politics of Unequal Benefits* (Berkeley: University of California Institute of International Studies, 1970).

15. Roland Ebel, "Governing the City State: Notes on the Politics of the Small Latin American Countries," *Journal of Inter-American Studies,* vol. 14 (August 1972), pp. 325–46; "Political Instability in Central America," *Current History* (February 1982), pp. 56ff.; "The Development and Decline of the Central American City State" in Wiarda, ed., *Rift and Revolution.*

16. These changes are treated in detail and on a country-by-country basis in Wiarda and Kline, *Latin American Politics.*

17. The evidence is thoroughly presented by Raúl Prebisch and in a series of reports issued by the UN's Economic Commission for Latin America.

18. Inter-American Development Bank, *Economic and Social Progress in Latin America: The External Sector* (Washington, D.C.: IADB, 1982).

19. The analysis is elaborated in Howard J. Wiarda, *Corporatism and National Development in Latin America* (Boulder, Colo.: Westview Press, 1981); and Wiarda and Kline, *Latin American Politics,* especially chapter 7.

20. Howard J. Wiarda, *Critical Elections and Critical Coups: State, Society and the Military in the Processes of Latin American Development* (Athens: Ohio University Center for International Studies, 1979).

21. The analysis follows that of Charles W. Anderson, *Politics and Economic Change in Latin America* (New York: Van Nostrand, 1967).

22. For the different perceptions of democracy in the two parts of the Americas see Howard J. Wiarda, "Democracy and Human Rights in Latin America: Toward a New Conceptualization," *Orbis,* vol. 22 (Spring 1978), pp. 137–60; and Wiarda, *The Continuing Struggle.*

23. The arguments are spelled out in greater detail in Wiarda, *Politics and Social Change.*

24. Charles D. Ameringer, *The Democratic Left in Exile: The Anti-Dictatorial Struggle in the Caribbean, 1945–59* (Miami: University of Miami Press, 1974).

25. Howard J. Wiarda, "Cuba," in Ben G. Burnett and Kenneth F. Johnson, eds., *Political Forces in Latin America* (Belmont, Calif.: Wadsworth, 1971), pp. 171–97.

26. Mark Falcoff, "Arms and Politics Revisited: Latin America as a Military and Strategic Theater," Paper prepared for the American Enterprise Institute's Public Policy Week panel of December 6–9, 1982; forthcoming in Howard J.

Wiarda, ed., *The Crisis in Latin America* (Washington, D.C.: American Enterprise Institute, 1984).

27. For a treatment of one such effort by a Caribbean state, see Howard J. Wiarda, "The Politics of Population Policy in the Dominican Republic," in Terry L. McCoy, ed., *The Dynamics of Population Policy in Latin America* (Cambridge, Mass.: Ballinger Press, 1974), pp. 293–322.

28. Mark Falcoff has written provocatively on this theme in his paper "Arms and Politics" and also in "How to Think about Cuba," *Washington Quarterly*, vol. 6 (Spring 1983), pp. 100–109.

29. The point is generally conceded by policy analysts; the debate has centered on what to do about it.

30. Mauricio García, "The Impact of Petrodollars on the Economy and the Public Sector of Venezuela," Paper presented at the Tenth National Meeting of the Latin American Studies Association, Washington, D.C., March 4, 1982.

31. Wolf Grabendorff, "The United States and Western Europe: Competition or Cooperation in Latin America," *International Affairs* (Autumn 1982), pp. 625–37.

32. The Center for Hemispheric Studies at the American Enterprise Institute, under a grant from the Tinker Foundation, is doing a book-length study of Iberian–Latin American relations.

33. J. C. M. Ogelsby, *Gringos from the Far North: Essays in the History of Canadian–Latin American Relations* (Toronto: Macmillan of Canada, 1976).

34. For a general treatment, see Robert O. Keohane and Joseph S. Nye, Jr., eds., *Trans-national Relations and International Politics* (Cambridge, Mass.: Harvard University Press, 1972).

35. Jiri Valenta, "The USSR, Cuba, and the Crisis in Central America," *Orbis* (Fall 1981), pp. 715–46.

36. The theme is elaborated in a major American Enterprise Institute research project on "American Vital Interests in Regions of Conflict," directed by Samuel P. Huntington and Brent Scowcroft.

37. For a discussion, see Howard J. Wiarda, "After Cancún: The United States and the Developing World," *PS*, vol. 15 (Winter 1982), pp. 40–48 (chapter 1 in this book).

38. Jeane J. Kirkpatrick, "The Hobbes Problem: Order, Authority, and Legitimacy in Central America," in *AEI Public Policy Papers* (Washington, D.C.: American Enterprise Institute, 1981).

39. The imagery is that of Juan José Arévalo, *The Shark and the Sardines* (New York: L. Stuart, 1961).

40. Howard J. Wiarda, "The Ethnocentrism of the Social Sciences: Implications for Research and Policy," *The Review of Politics*, vol. 43 (April 1981), pp. 163–67; and Howard J. Wiarda, "Toward a Non-Ethnocentric Theory of Development: Alternative Conceptions from the Third World," Paper presented at the Annual Meeting of the American Political Science Association, New York, September 3–6, 1981; also published in *Dados: Revista de Ciencias Sociais* (Brazil), vol. 25, no. 2 (1982), pp. 229–52, and in *Journal of Developing Areas* (July 1983).

CARL A. RUDISILL LIBRARY
LENOIR RHYNE COLLEGE

41. The issue is addressed more fully in chapter 2 in this book. "The United States and Latin America in the Aftermath of the Falklands/Malvinas Crisis," in *Latin America and the United States after the Falklands/Malvinas Crisis*—Hearings before the Subcommittee on Inter-American Affairs of the Committee on Foreign Affairs, House of Representatives, 97th Congress, 2d session, July 20 and August 5, 1982 (Washington, D.C.: GPO, 1982).

42. John E. Reilly, "The American Mood: A Foreign Policy of Self-Interest," *Foreign Policy*, no. 34 (Spring 1979), pp. 74–86.

43. As communicated to the Atlantic Council Working Group on Western Interests and U.S. Policy Options in the Caribbean.

44. The "new realities" of the Caribbean Basin and Latin America more generally, and their implications for U.S. policy, are elaborated in Howard J. Wiarda, "Conceptual and Political Dimensions of the Crisis in U.S.–Latin American Relations: Toward a New Policy Formulation," Paper prepared for the American Enterprise Institute's Public Policy Week panel of December 6–9, 1982; forthcoming in Wiarda, ed., *The Crisis in Latin America*.

45. Jerome Slater, *The OAS and United States Foreign Policy* (Columbus: Ohio State University Press, 1967); Gary Holten, "The UN and the OAS in the Dominican Republic Crisis: A Case Study of Globalism vs. Regionalism in Peace Keeping and Political Settlement" (Ph.D. diss.: University of Massachusetts, 1972).

46. Alejandro Orfila, "The Future of Inter-American Relations," Presentation made at the American Enterprise Institute, Washington, D.C., November 22, 1982.

47. See the discussion in Wiarda, "Cancún and After"; chapter 1 in this book.

48. Richard Feinberg with Robert Kennedy, "Western Interests and U.S. Policy Options in the Caribbean Basin: The Policy Paper" (Washington, D.C., Atlantic Council, 1983).

49. See also Wiarda, "Conceptual and Political Dimensions."

CARL A. RUDISILL LIBRARY
LENOIR RHYNE COLLEGE

7
At the Root of the Problem: Conceptual Failures in U.S.–Central American Relations

The *facts* about the crisis in Central America are sometimes unclear and often open to dispute. We disagree about whether El Salvador's civil war stems from internal factors or outside interference or the precise balance between these two, over whether Nicaragua is still somewhat pluralist or hopelessly Marxist-Leninist, over how much aid to give the area, what type of aid, to whom, and what the effects of past aid have been. These and other issues form the grist for our policy debate over Central America.

But, as suggested in the previous chapter, an at least equally important set of questions has to do with the concepts we use to interpret the area, the framework and models of understanding and analysis that we employ. Indeed, since it is largely on the basis of the models that we use that our assessments of the facts rest, one could argue that the conceptual problem is even more important than, and prior to, the factual ones. This chapter argues that that is precisely where our difficulties in understanding and coming to grips with the Central American imbroglio lie: The fact is that we have consistently used the wrong or inappropriate models to comprehend and interpret the area. And if our basic and fundamental interpretations have been wrong, it is small wonder that policy also has so often gone astray.

Basic Problems

At the root of the problem in U.S.–Latin American relations, we have argued, is our lack of knowledge and understanding of the area—what former Congressman James W. Symington referred to recently

Paper prepared for the Central American Project of the Carnegie Endowment for International Peace; see Robert S. Leiken, ed., *Central America: Anatomy of a Conflict* (Elmsford, N.Y.: Pergamon Press, 1984).

as "our fundamental, dogged, appalling ignorance of the Latin mind and culture."[1]

This lack of comprehension of Latin America, combined with an air of not a little scorn for its peoples and institutions, has long and complex origins.[2] It involves the historical sense of superiority that the northern, Protestant, and Anglo-Saxon nations have always harbored toward the southern, Catholic, and Latin societies; the idea that our country has been a success historically and Latin America a failure; the sense—now reinforced by social science concepts—that we are more developed and modern than they; even racial and ethnic prejudices concerning black, mulatto, and mestizo societies and peoples. This sense of superiority has further roots in the tradition of European political economy and sociology, in both Marxist and non-Marxist variants: That is, since Latin America had no industrialization, no capitalism, and no development, it therefore had no history. The sense has always been strong in Europe and the United States that Latin America is unworthy of serious study; that its culture and politics have nothing to contribute; that it can, therefore, be safely ignored until some major crisis—Guatemala in 1954, Cuba in the early 1960s, the Dominican Republic in 1965, Chile in 1973, and Central America now—forces it onto our television screens if not into our consciousness.

But the problem is not just a lack of understanding, which, incidentally, is mutual. Latin America's lack of understanding of us, we know, is at least as great as our lack of understanding of Latin America. The problem, however, is deeper than that. For not only do we not understand Latin America very well, but the fact is that we have very little desire to understand it better. We do not want to hear about it, we do not want to read about it, and our policy makers would much prefer that it disappear from our headlines and television screens and go back to being a "safe" area for U.S. interests.[3]

These problems of prejudice, condescension, and sense of superiority are especially acute regarding Central America. We may, grudgingly, admit some culture and worth in the larger South American countries of Argentina, Brazil, Chile, Colombia, or Venezuela, but those "banana republics" of Central America? That area provides the "stuff" of *New Yorker* cartoons and *opéra bouffe* stereotypes: comical, mustachioed men on horseback who gallop in and out of the presidential palace with frequent regularity. Central America is viewed as chaotic, disorganized, uninstitutionalized, dysfunctional, and wholly devoid of culture and civilization. Indeed, it is precisely because their politics are chronically unstable and devoid of institutions, coupled with the fact that they lie right on our doorstep, which accounts for the fact that the United States, in times of crisis, repeatedly becomes involved in the domestic and international affairs of the Central American countries.

Our attitudes toward Latin America in general, and toward Central America in particular, have been shaped not just by ephemeral biases and prejudices but by values and premises deeply ingrained in the American psyche. These values and premises permeate the prevailing political culture, and they are shared, albeit at different levels, by policy makers, theorists of development, and the general public.[4] The basic assumptions about third-world areas, in this case Central America, grow out of what Harvard historian Louis Hartz called "the liberal tradition in America."[5] The liberal tradition shapes and determines not only our domestic political debate but, more importantly for this paper, our foreign policy stance and attitudes as well. These premises are not always articulated as a formal and manifest ideology, but they are strongly held nonetheless and crucial in enabling us to understand attitudes and policy toward Central America. They constitute the intellectual baggage that American officials carry with them in thinking about foreign areas.

What are these prevailing attitudes that Hartz has called "liberal"? Essentially they stem from the liberal-Lockean premises of American democracy. These premises include a powerful predilection for stable, nonradical, constitutional, peaceful, republican-representative, and democratic governance. In the sense that Hartz uses the term, almost all American politicians and academics as well as the general public are thus "liberal": Richard Nixon as well as Hubert Humphrey, John Foster Dulles as well as Dean Acheson, Lyndon Johnson as well as John F. Kennedy, Ronald Reagan as well as Jimmy Carter. The question for our purposes, which have to do with foreign policy issues rather than domestic policy, is the one posed by Hartz: Can a country "born free" and "liberal," as the United States was, *ever* understand societies and polities where these premises do not apply? Or, as posed by Robert Packenham, who has written the best single study of the relations between the dominant American values and foreign policy: What happens when our liberal tradition confronts an obdurate foreign reality whose assumptions are often quite different, as in Central America?[6]

Conceptual Models and U.S.–Latin American Relations

Since World War II the United States has carried out a variety of major foreign aid programs, aimed initially at restoration in Western Europe and then at the underdeveloped areas of the third world. Latin America became the principal locus for much of these latter assistance efforts. During this same period American social scientists began theorizing about the processes of development in third-world nations. Again, Latin America received a major share of attention.

Neither the foreign policy initiatives nor the social science concepts that undergirded them were free of biases and value judgements. Both policy makers and social scientists, whether explicitly or implicitly, had definite ideas and preconceptions about what constituted good public policy in and toward the third world. These values closely reflected the prevailing ones in the American polity. They were based on the same liberal-Lockean notions that Hartz had identified as dominant within the American domestic political tradition. As applied to foreign policy and the third world, they implied an overriding emphasis on democracy, stability, anticommunism, peaceful and evolutionary political transitions, world community, and pro-Americanism.

It is not our purpose to criticize these values as values. They reflect, as stated, the prevailing American values, and they are also the preferred personal and political values of the author. The question is not these values per se but rather their relevance and appropriateness in Central America.

With regard specifically to U.S. foreign assistance programs, the dominant liberal-Lockean tradition had a pervasive influence. Based largely on the American experience, from which policy makers and social scientists alike largely drew their inspiration, the following four propositions help summarize the U.S. approach:[7]

1. *Change and development are easy.* All that is required is a tapping of the vast potential in other lands, the overcoming of traditional institutions, and the installation of the right party or government in power, and development will go forward. Little attention was devoted to the wrenching upheavals such changes imply, the blood and terror to which they often give rise, the frustrations of development and the possibilities, especially in weak and uninstitutionalized polities like those in Central America, not for progress but for fragmentation and breakdown.

2. *All good things go together.* That is, social modernization, economic growth, and political development can be pursued in concert. Little thought was given to the possibility that social modernization and economic growth might disrupt stability and political development rather than contributing to them, or that these features might not be complementary but contradictory instead. They have proven so in Central America.

3. *Stability must be maintained; radicalism and revolutionary regimes must be opposed.* But that idea seemed to be contradicted by the fact that many of the programs we fostered with the best of democratic intentions—agrarian reform, community development, and the like—might themselves be profoundly revolutionary and destabilizing. Our emphasis on evolutionary change, moreover, flew in the face of the obdurate opposition to *any* change in many nations (El Salvador's Fourteen Families, for instance) and the fact that in many countries only strong challenges to existing systems had the potential for achieving the kind of democratic and developmentalist changes we wanted.

4. *Distributing power is more important than accumulating power.* Our emphasis tended toward the support of pluralism and in favor of a separation of powers. In Central America as elsewhere in the third world, however, the basic problem is not to distribute power through community development and other programs; power in these societies is already fragmented. What is often required is to create strong central institutions where none have existed before, to concentrate power rather than disperse it.

In these liberal-Lockean propositions on which much of American policy toward the developing nations was based and in the brief qualifications introduced with each, one can already see the possibility for conflict, contradiction, and failure.

Implicit (and sometimes quite explicit) in the American foreign assistance programs, moreover, was a high degree of economic determinism. This too was based on the American experience of minimalist government involvement in development to allow the dynamic economic forces in the country to go forward on their own. One expression of this argument was W. W. Rostow's 1960 book *The Stages of Economic Growth,*[8] a volume that had a significant impact on the development literature then enjoying a major boom and on the U.S. foreign assistance programs. Rostow seemed to argue that economic forces were the determining ones in development, that political development (by which he meant democratization) inevitably flowed from economic growth, that change in the third world would inevitably follow the Western model, that such change could be fostered through U.S. economic aid, and that these changes were beneficent, universal, and unilinear, leading to polities closely resembling our own.

Another expression of the same view could be found in the work of Seymour M. Lipset[9] and Karl W. Deutsch[10] on the relations between economic development, social mobilization, and political development. They similarly focused on the economic and social prerequisites of democracy (economic development, literacy, and per capita radio and television) and suggested that democracy and pluralism were the inevitable result of prior socioeconomic modernization. Their error, which was usually more pronounced in their readers and followers (including policy makers) than in the original, quite careful formulations of these authors, was to mistake correlation for causation, to assume that since most democracies in the world were often the most economically developed, the latter was the *cause* of the former. It followed, based on this assumption, that political democracy and development (in most of the literature the terms were used synonomously) would be a product of economic development and that their growth would proceed inevitably from the motor force of economic growth. In these ways scholars such as Rostow, Lipset, and Deutsch came to be known as "Dr. Yes" spokesmen for the U.S. foreign assistance programs designed in the early 1960s.

The Rostow-Lipset-Deutsch view was quite congenial to U.S. foreign aid administrators and economists—and not just because in the mid-1960s Rostow, himself an economist, was the chief White House foreign policy adviser and thus in a position to put his ideas into practice. It also corresponded closely to the technocratic and generally apolitical preferences of officials of the newly created Agency for International Development, again largely dominated by economists who preferred, for professional as well as for career reasons, to concentrate on the seemingly easy task of economic aid and to avoid so far as possible the vexing, messy, difficult political variables that seemed always to "get in the way." One suspects that economists and aid officials would almost always prefer to relegate what are in fact difficult political issues and choices to the subcategory of "dependent variables" because (1) they are too indeterminate for their taste and (2) they tend to interfere with the neat econometric models on which the profession would prefer to make its predictions.

From these major assumptions, biases, and predilections, all strongly ingrained in the American political culture as well as in the formulations of social scientists and policy makers, a number of subassumptions and specific policy initiatives flowed. A brief review of some of them will illustrate the argument. These assumptions are important because they still often dominate the thinking behind the U.S. assistance programs.

1. *The emphasis on economic development.* Simply put, the rationale of a large part of the U.S. economic assistance program in the last quarter century, based on the assumptions and literature already presented, has been that if only we can pour in sufficient economic aid,

political stability and democracy, as well as anticommunism, will inevitably result. The difficulties with this proposition are many. For example, Costa Rica developed as a democracy before U.S. aid was proferred and not as a result of that aid. In other countries where the U.S. assistance programs were considerable—the Dominican Republic in the early 1960s, for example, or Chile in the later 1960s—it would be difficult to argue that stability and democracy flowed necessarily or immediately from economic growth. In some of these countries, in fact, just the opposite result was produced: Economic development helped stimulate greater and even revolutionary expectations, social fragmentation set in, violence increased, the military stepped in, repression increased, and radical revolutionary appeals found new receptivity.

It would be hard to argue that economic development in Nicaragua led to much of either democracy or stability; rather, the growth that occurred tended principally to strengthen the Somoza dictatorship—until other events overwhelmed Somoza and led to the victory of the Sandinistas, and one would have to stretch one's definition a great deal to call that a stable or democratic regime. One would be equally hard pressed to argue that U.S.-backed economic growth anywhere else in Central America—El Salvador, Guatemala, or Honduras—has led inevitably, unilinearly, or even by fits and starts, to democracy, stability, or moderate, progressive, and pro-American regimes. One need not necessarily accept the author's admitted biases about economists to recognize from the Central American experience that something is quite wrong with much social science and foreign policy development theory that posits a direct and positive relationship between economic development and either democracy or stability.[11]

2. *The role of the middle class.* Much of our development assistance has been based on the prevailing social science idea that a large middle class will be a bastion of stability, progress, democracy, and anticommunism, as it is in the United States and Western Europe. Hence, much of our assistance to Central America over the past two decades was aimed at building up this middle class. The big assumption here is that the middle class in Central America will behave like its North American counterpart, with moderation, pragmatism, responsibility, and so forth.

There is no doubt, of course, that the middle class has grown in numbers in Central America, but the expected social and political concomitants of that growth have not followed. The evidence we have seems to indicate that the Central American middle class is not happily middle-of-the-road and democratic but tends to imitate the behavior of the traditional oligarchies; that it is exceedingly conscious of its newly won place and position in the society and tends to disdain the lower classes; that it has often supported military takeovers to prevent the lower classes from gaining a share of power; that it is not necessarily progressive and modernizing but often reactionary; and that instead of being a force for stability, it has helped precipitate fragmentation and instability.[12] The Central American middle class has not become a moderate and progressive influence or a bulwark of democracy, nor is there much evidence even that the trends are inevitably in that direction. Another of the main assumptions of the U.S. assistance programs in the past twenty years, therefore, has been shown to be without much real foundation in fact, in terms of actual behavior as compared with theoretical assumptions.

3. *Trade union development.* Another of the assumptions on which U.S. assistance has been based is that through our economic aid we could help create a moderate, progressive, democratic, and anticommunist trade unionism in Central America and elsewhere. Once again the model is the generally nonpolitical, nonideological trade unionism of the United States. Here one can again see the persistent preference for technocratic solutions that eschew any connection with partisan politics or even, one might say, the real nuts-and-bolts issues of Central American life. A moderate trade unionism, it is argued, would support moderate democracies and serve as a further defense against right-wing coups on the one hand or Communist seizures of power on the other.

In fact, the growth of trade unionism in Central America has frequently helped precipitate coups on the part of the armed forces who tend to see the labor unions as potential rivals to their own institutional dominance. In some cases the unions, including at times those supported by the United States, have urged or helped the military to stage coups against more radical elements. Nor has a nonpolitical, nonideological trade unionism resulted; one could argue in fact that the opposite has occurred—perhaps inevitably given Central America's history of ideological and intensely *political* trade unionism as compared with the nonpolitical trade unionism of the United States.[13] Furthermore, a nonpolitical but anti-Communist trade unionism is a contradiction in terms, and to our consternation we have not always been able to have it both ways in Central America.

Admittedly, scholars might honestly reach different assessments and conclusions regarding the U.S. effort to transfer its brand of trade unionism to Central America, and there is evidence that in recent years the efforts of U.S. labor and its international arm, the American Institute for Free Labor Development, have changed in major ways.

But enough has been said to indicate the U.S. models of trade unionism and collective bargaining have not always worked well or as intended in Central America, they have sometimes worked at cross-
purposes with other aspects of U.S. policy, and scant evidence exists
that at any time soon will the Central American unions follow the U.S.
example *or* serve as complementary strongholds of stability, democracy, and anticommunism.

4. *The military as professional and apolitical.* Over the past thirty
years, U.S. military assistance programs in Central America, in accord
with the economic and other assistance programs mentioned earlier,
have been aimed at creating armed forces that are professionalized,
apolitical, oriented toward civic action, democratic, and anti-Communist. The problems with this effort have been many. To begin with, the
second and fifth items in the list are often incompatible: A military,
like a labor federation, cannot be apolitical and anti-Communist at
one and the same time. The first and fourth items may be similarly
incompatible, for the fact is that the greater professionalization of the
military in this region has led not to fewer but to more usurpations of
power and to longer periods of military rule.[14] The new training that
the armed forces have received in development economics, modern
management, and national security doctrine has led them to con-
clude—with considerable reason—that they can run their countries
better than the civilians.

Nor have the efforts aimed at involving the Central American
militaries in civic action programs worked well, since those tasks involve the officers getting their hands dirty, leaving the amenities of
the capital city for the discomforts of the provinces, participating in
programs directed toward the public weal rather than toward their
own private enrichment, and in general violating long-established
cultural norms concerning appropriate behavior for the proud military
institution. Many of the same qualifiers apply to U.S. efforts to get the
military in El Salvador to carry the fight to the guerrillas, to cease
violating their own people's human rights, and to give up their historical practice of supplementing their meager salaries by strong-arm
methods and illegal business ventures. Not only have these efforts not
proved successful, but there is little evidence that the American assistance programs are sufficiently responsive to the society and culture
they are dealing with to offer the military needed but alternative in-
centives.

One could easily expand this discussion of U.S. aid programs to
cover agrarian reform, community development, family planning, bureaucratic modernization, tax reform, and a host of others. What is

striking about these programs is the degree to which all of them are based upon the American (and secondarily the Western European) experience and model of development. They are all predicated on the notion of an inevitable, unilinear evolution toward a stable, bourgeois, happy, Lockean-liberal, democratic, and middle-of-the-road society and polity that, perhaps not surprisingly, looks just like ours. Whether any of the main facets of that strategy have any prospect for success, however, let alone a very strong prospect, in Central America where the societal norms and behavioral expectations are quite different from our own, is another story entirely.

Let us see how these assumptions and expectations have worked out in specific U.S. aid programs.

How the Wrong Models Often Lead Us Astray

In reviewing the history of U.S. assistance programs in Central America since World War II, one is struck by how consistent—and, our argument is, how consistently misapplied—they have been. From Truman to the present administration and at all times in between, the assumptions have consistently been the liberal-Lockean ones discussed earlier. Nuances and changes of emphases have occurred in each new administration, but the basic assumptions have been the same: If only we could pour in sufficient funds and American know-how, we could modernize these economies, create a stable middle class, professionalize the armed forces, build democracy, create apolitical trade unions, guarantee stability, and all the rest—all at once. These programs have been breathtaking in their sweep and characteristically American in their optimism and ethnocentrism. The current crisis, fragmentation, and breakdown in Central America, however, would seem to be the best evidence that the theory and assumptions are in need of thorough reexamination.[15]

The Truman Doctrine. While the message of the Truman Doctrine of March 12, 1947, was aimed at the Soviet Union, its economic assistance provisions were intended for the benefit of Greece and Turkey. Its rationale was not purely humanitarian but rather the U.S. national interest: the prevention of possible destabilization and Communist takeovers. In Greece the United States organized elections with the hope that the democratic centrist parties would prevail, stability would be ensured, and a progressive development plan would be carried out. The economic development plans were aimed at producing political order and reducing the appeals of communism.

The efforts to prevent a Communist victory were successful in the short term, but the rest of the program was less so. It had been a sweeping and grandiose program, a grand strategy involving economic aid, military assistance, and political development (that is, democracy). Like other American assistance programs to come, it assumed that change and development were easy, that all they required were American money and expertise, that, since all good things go together, political democracy would result from economic growth, and that everything would work out in the end since the Turks and the Greeks, presumably, shared the same values as we. The long-term result merits considerable skepticism that U.S. efforts could either engineer democracy or secure stability in Greece and Turkey, or that those countries would develop inevitably in our mold if sufficient economic aid were forthcoming.[16]

The Marshall Plan. The Marshall Plan had much the same rationale and was part of the same larger strategy as the Truman Doctrine: Political development was contingent on economic assistance. Although the instruments of policy were almost exclusively economic, the goals were strategic and political and assumed to flow from the economic: stability, democracy, pro-Americanism, anticommunism, and the establishment of centrist regimes and movements.

The distinctive feature of the Marshall Plan, of course, was that its main goals were achieved, within the specified four-year time period and considerably below the dollar amount appropriated by Congress. When essentially the same plans and programs were tried out later in Central America and other third-world countries, however, they did not work. The difference was that Western Europe already had the indigenous institutions, parties, and leadership to carry out a major redevelopment program. The real need in Europe was for temporary economic assistance, and when the United States made that assistance available, democracy and stability were quickly achieved. Perhaps nowhere else, as Packenham argues, were the conditions so propitious for the approach that based political development on economic development. Those same conditions had not been present in Greece and Turkey, and they would not be present in Asia, Africa, or Latin America.

Point Four. President Truman had announced the Point Four Program in his 1949 inaugural address. Point Four represented an effort to transfer the ideas of the Marshall Plan to the underdeveloped world. Again the notion was that economic aid and American technical assistance would bring freedom, democracy, pro-Americanism, stability, international understanding, anticommunism, and the end of war.

The list of objectives was thus expanded, but the same assumptions underlay the program.

Point Four failed to achieve the goals desired not because the idea of using American knowledge and assistance was wrong but because of its exaggerated statements of what could thereby be accomplished politically. It failed to appraise realistically the difficulty of achieving change and development in the emerging nations and to assess accurately the relations between economic and political development. Rather than leading to stability and democracy, economic development, we now know, has the potential to undermine both. These misperceptions were part of the same, continuous effort outlined earlier to export liberal-Lockean presumptions and institutions to societies where they did not fit or fit only partly. They illustrate again the American proclivity to assume that the U.S. developmental experience, or that of Western Europe under the Marshall Plan, has the same relevance in the third world and in quite different cultural areas.

The Alliance for Progress. The economic achievements of John F. Kennedy's Alliance for Progress were considerable. The pace of change was accelerated throughout Central America in the 1960s and on into the early 1970s, per capita income was raised considerably, new industries grew up, the Central American Common Market was launched, and several of the economies of the area "took off." Economic growth in turn stimulated greater social modernization: Roads and houses were built, education improved, sanitation and health care advanced, agriculture developed, and so on.

The political goals of the Alliance, however, which were the main reasons the program had been launched in the first place, were not achieved. The Central American middle class, as we have seen, has not developed as a stronghold of democracy and stability. The armed forces have not become both more professionalized and subservient to civilian authority. The trade unions have not become more moderate and apolitical. Economic development did not produce political development. The elites have not evidenced a greater sense of noblesse oblige or responsibility. Indeed, if the basic goals of U.S. policy were—and remain—to secure moderate, stable, pro-American regimes throughout the area, the present situation of conflict, guerrilla challenges, and civil wars must surely make one question the degree of success. Thus, while the economic and social achievements of the Alliance were considerable, its assumptions concerning fundamental political development have proved wrong.

Several reasons may be suggested for the failure of the political agenda of the Alliance. First, the program and its possibilities were exaggerated and oversold; the ambitious goals set forth were both unachievable and, in several areas, internally contradictory. Second, the Alliance was based on economic determinist assumptions derived from the Rostowian-Lipsetonian literature on development then also current that, we have already seen, was logically flawed and ignored crucial political and cultural differences. Third, the model of a happy, liberal, middle-class, yeoman-farmer (hence the motivation for agrarian reform), socially just, pluralistic, and democratic society and polity were all derived from the United States and had little to do with Central America. Fourth, the mechanism relied on so heavily, the Central American Common Market, was based too much on the European Marshall Plan concept. The common market worked well in Western Europe because the two principal economies involved, the French and the German, were closely complementary; but in Central America the economies were all competitive rather than complementary, and hence the common market produced only limited successes. Political rivalries also tore the CACM apart. Fifth, Central America is a classic case of how U.S. aid policies and modernization helped break down existing and traditional institutions (family and kinship groups, patronage networks, clan groups, and patron-client patterns) without creating anything viable to replace them, thus helping precipitate the instability that now plagues U.S. policy in the area.

Carter's Campaign for Human Rights. President Carter had initiated a vigorous campaign in defense of human rights. There was for a time, and as a result of the Carter policies, less use of torture as an instrument of power. In addition, quite a number of political prisoners were freed, some lives were saved, and some of the more atrocious abuses of human rights were prevented. These are certainly not small accomplishments.

On the other hand, the campaign was carried out in a naive missionary style reminiscent of Woodrow Wilson. U.S. criteria for human rights were the only standards used, and the program all too often ethnocentrically reflected the U.S. civil rights movement of the 1960s. It was applied haphazardly, inconsistently, and not always impartially. By its sometimes gross and indiscriminate condemnations of whole countries or whole governments, the policy produced numerous backlashes. It turned otherwise friendly governments against us and often united their nationalistic peoples behind an unacceptable regime only because we had attacked it. And like so many of the overblown and oversold programs we have chronicled, in the final analysis its successes and accomplishments were rather modest compared to the effort expended and the costs incurred.[17]

Project Democracy. Project Democracy is really two different programs, or more accurately, two different conceptions of the same program. One group of its adherents favors a grandiose plan to bring democracy to Central America—political parties like our own, honest and competitive elections, competitive and pluralistic interest groups, the full gamut of representative institutions, and the social programs of an advanced industrial society—and apparently believes both that the United States can so export its institutions to other nations *and* that Central America wishes to recast itself entirely in the institutional arrangements of the United States. The second group has a much more modest agenda, involving stepped-up cultural exchanges, a limited amount of assistance to appropriate Central American groups, and some restrained nudges by the United States, where appropriate, in favor of democratic outcomes and human rights.

The first approach seems altogether unrealistic.[18] The notion that by our aid we in the United States can entirely reorient societies and cultures cast in molds quite different from our own is preposterous. Not only can we not do it but they, the Central Americans, do not want it. While they prefer democratic, representative institutions, they are doubtful whether these work very well in their own fractured situations, and they much prefer representative democratic institutions in accord with their own history and traditions to those imported from abroad. There are even doubts as to our capacity to assist the Latin Americans in *their own* aspirations and struggles for democracy, a strategy that may produce some results in the bigger and better-institutionalized countries of South America but has a very limited possibility for success in the personalistic and less-institutionalized societies of Central America.

Clearly, the more modest agenda is preferable and more appropriate. Even that option, though, faces major difficulties. In the first place, the idea remains powerful in the Department of State, the Agency for International Development, the Department of Defense, and elsewhere that we know best for Central America, that given the area's own apparent incapacities, we can solve the problems of those countries for them. Ethnocentrism is still pervasive within the U.S. government and can easily overwhelm even the best-designed U.S. assistance programs involving real input by the Central Americans themselves.

In the second place, the temptation to support a stronger prodemocracy option, even if the possibilities for success in Central America are modest, is almost irresistible within the U.S. government. The Congress is in favor, the press is in favor, the intellectuals are in favor, the bureaucracy is in favor, and major U.S. interest groups are in favor.

In addition, a strong prodemocracy program abroad enables an administration to stand for the "right and good things," to present a unified, coherent, and publicly acceptable program to the voters and to take away some major arguments from its opposition. These are all nearly insurmountable reasons for pursuing a stronger stance in favor of democracy than may be realistic or called for. But note all these impulses toward a stronger prodemocracy position have obvious roots in U.S. domestic politics and not necessarily any strong basis in the realities of Central America. That in fact is the chief cause of so many failures in the litany of policies pursued by the United States in Central America.

A Marshall Plan for Central America. I strongly support a major program of social and economic assistance to Central America but wish to caution against exaggerated expectations that cannot be fulfilled and may, hence, lead to even greater dissatisfaction throughout the area. In addition, there are major problems with the Marshall Plan idea that need to be resolved. First, it remains quite a vague proposal; none of its specifics has so far been announced. Second, it is a long-term proposition on which there is likely to be considerable agreement, but in the meantime the difficult and immediate security and political issues of the region, on which there is far more discord, will still need to be addressed. A third problem is that the Congress may well not go along with a new, large-scale foreign assistance program. Or it may gut the program in much the same way it gutted the earlier Caribbean Basin Initiative in many of its key provisions. Furthermore, the U.S. public is strongly opposed to more foreign aid. Such a program will be especially difficult to pass if it means that U.S. jobs will be sacrificed for the sake of greater access to our markets for Central American products.

Most of all, however, one fears that the lessons of the past have not been learned. The Marshall Plan idea is being spoken of in some quarters as almost a panacea for Central America's ills. While we can certainly assist, nudge, and cajole, the fact remains that we cannot solve Central America's problems for it. In addition, any such Marshall Plan for Central America, we hope, would not be based on the same unwarranted assumptions of the Alliance for Progress, such as the faith in the middle class as a stable and progressive force. Finally, we need to recognize the basic differences between the nations of Western Europe following World War II and those of Central America today and the reasons that a Marshall Plan could succeed so well in the former and prove far more problematic in the latter. Once again, the heart of the problem would seem to lie in the conceptual frame-

116

works that we use and their relevance and appropriateness in the Central American context.

Elements of a Central American Model of Development

We have been quite critical of past U.S. policies in Central America; the question now remains as to the base on which sounder policies can be grounded.

In general terms, policy toward Central America requires a more realistic, prudent, consistent, and pragmatic basis than in the past.[19] That involves four overall strategies: (1) taking Central America seriously for the first time; (2) having appropriate modesty regarding what we can reasonably expect to accomplish in Central America; (3) understanding Central America in terms of its own institutional standards and practices; and (4) casting aside that pervasive ethnocentrism that, we have seen, has been so strongly present in all the U.S. initiatives toward Central America going back to the immediate post-World War II period and even much earlier (when a wayward early U.S. envoy thought that he could best travel to Central America by way of Buenos Aires and, having finally arrived in Central America, did not know where he was and could find "no government" to whom to present his credentials).

Taking Central America seriously for the first time means that we treat it not as a collection of banana republics, that we not be condescending and patronizing, that we understand and come to grips with its own political dynamics rather than imposing our preferred solution upon it, that we appreciate that Central American society and politics can be as complex and systematic as our own, that we work through the existing institutions and systems of the area rather than trying to substitute some other ones that cannot and will not work, and that we look on its developmental goals with sympathy and understanding.

Having appropriate modesty regarding what we can reasonably expect to accomplish in Central America means that we eschew grand but unrealistic designs, that we comprehend realistically the social and cultural forces holding back change as well as those forces promoting it, that we avoid raising expectations so high that they cannot possibly be fulfilled and therefore give rise both to strong disappointments and to even greater pressures for sweeping revolution, and that we avoid casting aside workable (in that context) traditional institutions.

Points 3 and 4, understanding Central America in terms of its own institutional practices and avoiding ethnocentrism, are really the opposite sides of the same coin. The author has written at length on these themes,[20] and need not repeat all those materials here. Some elements of the case for a nonethnocentric theory of development need to be presented, however, to show how a more realistic, empathetic, and workable policy can be fashioned.

For example, in focusing on the Central American middle class, we need to know how and why that middle class is different from the Western European and the North American ones and why it does not seem to provide a bulwark for democracy and stability in Central America as it does in these other areas. We must similarly understand the politicized nature of trade unionism in Central America and its differences from the apolitical, collective-bargaining model of the United States. At the other end of the social scale, we are woefully ill-equipped to comprehend elite political behavior in Central America, the nature of extended family relationships that often serve as substitutes for political parties, the nature of clan rivalries and competition, and the dynamics of elite circulations in power.

We need to understand further how greater assistance to the armed forces in Central America and increased professionalization may lead to more military involvement in politics rather than less. We do not comprehend well the consideration of social status within the Central American officer corps, the motives for seeking an officership, or the definition of acceptable officer behavior; therefore, we are unable to provide an adequate incentive system for the officers when we want them to pursue a vigorous antiguerrilla strategy.

Nor do we understand the tentative, as distinct from definitive, mandate that elections carry, or their frequent function as devices to ratify an existing regime rather than as means to allow genuine choices. We fail to appreciate the role of the army as virtually a fourth branch of government in Central America—and all that that designation implies. We know little about state-society relations in that area, which are quite different from American-style interest group relations; and we have little understanding of the essentially corporative nature of these relations as distinct from the free-wheeling pluralist form they take in the United States.

Even the terms we use have quite different meanings. Such basic concepts as *democracy, representation, rights, separation of powers,* and *popular sovereignty* all mean something quite different in Central America from what they mean in the United States. There is little evidence that U.S. policy makers or the leaders of either of the two political parties understand such differences or, when they do understand them, that they do so empathetically. Rather, our inclination is to dismiss the Central American meaning of these terms as a sign of inferiority or underdevelopment and to substitute our own presumably superior notions and interpretations for them. Not only do we often fail to understand Central America in terms of its own institutional arrangements, therefore, but when we do, we seek to replace them with presumably more developed kinds that consistently bear a striking resemblance to our own institutional preferences. Policies based on that sort of thinking have not worked in the past, and they are unlikely to achieve better results in the future.

Conclusion

American policy toward Central America, it is almost universally agreed, has not registered many clear successes. There is much discussion of the reasons for the many failures and the National Bipartisan (Kissinger) Commission on Central America was created in large part to suggest new approaches distinct from the perceived failures of policy in the past.

It has been suggested here that the key reason for our poverty of policy in Central America derives from the poverty of the theories undergirding them. Consistently, in both Democratic and Republican administrations, we have applied the wrong or inappropriate models in Central America. These include models of economic development, models of military behavior, models of political change, and models of class or group interaction. These models were based almost exclusively on the Western European and U.S. experiences and had little to do with the realities, history, and internal dynamics of Central America. The models used were not only overly rigid, ethnocentric, and naive, but also they undermined many existing and transitional institutions and thus contributed further to the very instability our policies have consistently sought to prevent.

The possibility exists that we may now begin to break with the formulas used in the past. There are hints of such possibilities in the younger generation of Foreign Service officers, among Latin American specialists, and in the hearings before and papers presented to the Kissinger Commission.[21] At the same time strong resistance to such changes exists in Congress, the foreign policy bureaucracies, several powerful interest groups and lobbies, and public opinion. Unless we begin to treat Central America seriously, however, on its own terms, in its own institutional context, with empathy, and without the condescension and ethnocentrism of the past, then the new and worthwhile policy proposals recently put forward, such as Project Democracy, a

Marshall Plan for Central America, and other quite reasonable suggestions offered in the reports of the Atlantic Council and the Kissinger Commission,[22] have almost no possibility of achieving success.

Notes

1. James W. Symington, "Learn Latin America's Culture," *New York Times*, September 23, 1983.

2. See, for example, David M. Potter, *People of Plenty: Economic Abundance and the American Character* (Chicago: University of Chicago Press, 1954); Daniel J. Boorstin, *The Genius of American Politics* (Chicago: University of Chicago Press, 1953); Charles Gibson, ed., *The Black Legend: Anti-Spanish Attitudes in the Old World and the New* (New York: Knopf, 1971); and Reginald Horsman, *Race and Manifest Destiny: The Origins of American Racial Anglo-Saxonism* (Cambridge: Harvard University Press, 1981).

3. See especially chapters 2, 3, and 5.

4. Donald J. Devine, *The Political Culture of the United States* (Boston, Mass.: Little, Brown, 1972).

5. Louis Hartz, *The Liberal Tradition in America: An Interpretation of American Political Thought since the Revolution* (New York: Harcourt, Brace and World, 1955).

6. Robert Packenham, *Liberal America and the Third World: Political Development Ideas in Foreign Aid and Social Science* (Princeton, N.J.: Princeton University Press, 1973).

7. The discussion follows that of Packenham, *Liberal America*, p. 20; but see also Samuel P. Huntington, *Political Order in Changing Societies* (New Haven, Conn.: Yale University Press, 1968).

8. W. W. Rostow, *The Stages of Economic Growth: A Non-Communist Manifesto* (Cambridge: Cambridge University Press, 1960).

9. Seymour M. Lipset, "Some Social Requisites of Democracy: Economic Development and Political Legitimacy," *American Political Science Review*, vol. 53 (March 1959), pp. 69–105.

10. Karl W. Deutsch, "Social Mobilization and Political Development," *American Political Science Review*, vol. 55 (September 1961), pp. 493–514.

11. The theme of the disjuncture between economic growth and political development has been forcefully argued by Huntington, *Political Order*.

12. The controversy over the role of the middle classes in Latin America has generated a good deal of discussion. The classic statement of the "salvation through the middle class" scenario is John J. Johnson, *Political Change in Latin America: The Emergence of the Middle Sectors* (Stanford, Calif.: Stanford University Press, 1958). For a valuable exchange of views see the discussion between Robert J. Alexander, James Petras, and Victor Alba in *New Politics* (Winter 1962) and (Winter 1965).

13. The literature includes Robert J. Alexander, *Organized Labor in Latin America* (New York: Free Press, 1965); Victor Alba, *Politics and the Labor Move-*

ment in Latin America (Stanford, Calif.: Stanford University Press, 1968); and Howard J. Wiarda, "The Corporative Origins of the Iberian and Latin American Labor Relations Systems," *Studies in Comparative International Development,* vol. 13 (Spring 1978), pp. 3–37.

14. See Alfred Stepan, *The Military in Politics: Changing Patterns in Brazil* (Princeton, N.J.: Princeton University Press, 1971).

15. The argument here and in the following five paragraphs derives from Packenham, *Liberal America.*

16. The best analysis is William Hardy McNeill, *Greece: American Aid in Action, 1947–1956* (New York: Twentieth Century Fund, 1957). In reviewing the literature on the Greek civil war, 1947–1949, and the American response to it, one is struck by the remarkable parallels with El Salvador in the early 1980s.

17. A careful and balanced assessment is Larman C. Wilson, "Human Rights in United States Foreign Policy: The Rhetoric and the Practice," in Donald C. Piper and Ronald C. Terchek, eds., *Interaction: Foreign Policy and Public Policy* (Washington, D.C.: American Enterprise Institute, 1983), pp. 178–208.

18. For a longer—and stronger—critique see Howard J. Wiarda, "Can Democracy Be Exported? The Quest for Democracy in United States Latin American Policy," Paper prepared for the Inter-American Dialogue on U.S.–Latin American Relations in the 1980s, sponsored by the Woodrow Wilson International Center for Scholars, Washington, D.C., March 1983, and forthcoming in a volume edited by Kevin Middlebrook and Carlos Rico.

19. For elaboration, see the concluding chapter of this volume.

20. Especially, by the author, *Critical Elections and Critical Coups: State, Society, and the Military in the Processes of Latin American Development* (Athens: Center for International Studies, Ohio University, 1979); *The Continuing Struggle for Democracy in Latin America* (Boulder, Colo.: Westview Press, 1980); with Harvey F. Kline, *Latin American Politics and Development* (Boston, Mass.: Houghton-Mifflin, 1979); *Corporatism and National Development in Latin America* (Boulder, Colo.: Westview Press, 1981); and *Politics and Social Change in Latin America: The Distinct Tradition,* 2d rev. ed. (Amherst: University of Massachusetts Press, 1982).

21. The author's presentation before the commission summarized many of these findings; see his "U.S. Policy in Central America: Toward a New Relationship," Statement presented to the National Bipartisan Commission on Central America, United States Department of State, Washington, D.C., September 28–29, 1983; chapter 8 in this book.

22. The Atlantic Council's recommendations were contained in a policy paper prepared by its study group on "Western Interests and U.S. Policy Options in the Caribbean Basin"; see also the background papers prepared for the council by David Scott Palmer, Sidney Weintraub, Jack Child, and Howard J. Wiarda (chapter 6 in this book), forthcoming in a volume to be published under Council auspices. The Kissinger Commission report was issued in early 1984.

8

U.S. Policy in Central America: Toward a New Relationship

The United States has in the past accorded little attention to Central America. Not only do we not understand that area very well, but we have seldom tried to understand it. Our notions about Central America are shrouded in myths and stereotypes. Attitudes in the United States toward the region tend to be patronizing, condescending, and lacking in empathy. We refer to the nations of the area as "banana republics" and doubt if they are worthy of serious attention, culturally, historically, politically, sociologically. We turn our attention to the area only in times of crisis, and then our inclination is to look for an easy formula, pat solutions. We refuse to take Latin America seriously, on its own terms or in all its multifaceted complexity.[1]

This chapter fills in some gaps in our general understanding of Central America, assesses the difficulties of development there, provides an overview of the new realities of the area and of the constraints on U.S. policy as it attempts to come to terms with the area, and evaluates policy options and possibilities.[2]

Four points need to be addressed initially. First, though the assignment of the Commission was to focus on the mid-term (three to five years) to the longer term (ten to twenty years), it needs to be recognized that in practice these time frames cannot be easily separated. This presentation follows the instructions given: it does not deal with current events but concentrates on presenting models and frames of reference for longer-term policy. However, one must understand the element of artificiality in such a strict division. For one thing Central America today remains very much a prisoner of its earlier history and many of its main institutions will likely continue in that earlier mold; for another, it is impossible to conceive that Central America three, five, ten, or twenty years hence will not be affected by what is occurring there now; and third, keeping in mind this past

Statement prepared for the National Bipartisan Commission on Central America, U.S. Department of State, Washington, D.C., September 28–29, 1983.

122

history, one doubts that in the near or even longer term Central America will be altered in its fundamentals by what U.S. policy makers choose to do. The heavy hand of history in that area shapes the present and the future too decisively for these time frames to serve as more than reference points or for our efforts to effect basic change. We can have a marginal effect in that area, but we cannot reverse the course of history. However, as former Senate Foreign Relations Committee Chief of Staff Pat Holt has remarked, "Even a change of direction of 3–4 percent would have been enough to save the *Titanic*."[3]

A second point has to do with the presumption on which the work of this Commission was based. It is widely believed that since past U.S. policies have "failed," there is now need for a new approach. That, after all, is why the Commission was created. We would be remiss, however, in branding all past U.S. policies in Central America failures and therefore in opting for some wholesale—and hence probably impractical—revamping of policy. Although this chapter does suggest a new formula and some new approaches, these build upon earlier efforts, reflecting and adjusting to the new realities of the area, rather than any sweeping and unrealistic abandonment of past strategies. Such an abrupt departure may seem tempting, but it may well not work; and I am not entirely convinced that past policies were the unmitigated disaster that is often claimed.

Third, we must warn against the possibility that the Commission might be overly tempted by some pat and easy formula. Among the possibilities are the Project Democracy and new Marshall Plan ideas. These are useful ideas deserving of support, but there is reason to be skeptical of formulas that promise all-encompassing solutions to Central America's problems and thus raise exaggerated expectations.[4]

Fourth, we must bear in mind that what is really needed is a careful, serious, bipartisan strategy, as distinct from an unbalanced and intensely partisan one. Many axes—partisan, personal, academic, political, institutional—are being ground over the issue of Central America but these controversies do little to bring us closer to a genuine understanding of the area. Particularly in the midst of an election campaign, the temptations to partisanship, or to the private and personal ambitions that Harvard's Edward Banfield called "private-regardingness" (as distinct from "public regardingness"), are powerful.[5] In this charged atmosphere, it is especially important to suggest recommendations that are balanced and prudent, that have realistic possibilities of generating support and of achieving success rather than extreme, partisan, unrealistic and impractical ones. The presentation of such a reasonable, balanced, nonpartisan, and prudent policy is what I have attempted here.

Political Institutions and Institutionalization in Central America

The literature on political institutions and institutionalization in developing countries is rich and diverse, but little of it has been applied to Central America. The seminal book on the subject is Samuel P. Huntington's *Political Order in Changing Societies*.[6] This book abounds with general ideas and broad concepts but has almost nothing to say about Central America. Indeed, one would be hard pressed to think of any general volume in that body of literature called "political development" that contains anything more than passing reference to the area.

The problem for Central America—and for U.S. policy there—is an almost complete lack of institutions of any sort. During Spain's 300-year-long rule Central America was characterized by colonial neglect. In contrast to Mexico, for example, the Central American nations never developed a system of strong, centralized political authority, a strong and centralized military, an efficient and rationalized bureaucracy, a strong Church, or even a strong oligarchy that might have held these countries together after independence.[7] Nor did the institutions of a liberal polity—political parties, electoral machinery, republican and representative institutions—develop in nineteenth-century Central America.[8]

The result was—and is—a group of countries in Central America, Costa Rica being the foremost exception, with the institutional infrastructures neither of a traditional nor of a liberal-democratic polity. Central America was undefined institutionally, unformed—and it remains so. Indeed, at the heart of the problem in Central America— and at the root of its instability, violence, and lack of viability—is the absence of any kind of institutions capable of holding the society and polity together, let alone of carrying out effective programs. The absence of institutions, particularly of a democratic sort, makes it difficult for the United States to assist these countries, to grasp the levers and to turn them to positive developmental goals.

To compensate for these institutional deficiencies—what the Central Americans often refer to as a *falta de civilización*—a variety of other agencies has been created over time. These seldom conform to U.S. or Western notions of good and proper governance, but historically they have not functioned entirely badly in the Central American context. These indigenous institutions include extended family networks, clan and patronage networks, mixed civil-military regimes that defy the rigid classificatory schemes we often employ to define a government as either the one or the other, personalistic and populist regimes such as that of former President Torrijos in Panama. Such regimes are seldom fully democratic by our lights, but they are seldom fully totalitarian either. Given the small, personalistic, city-state nature of the Central American polities, such "mixed" regimes may not be entirely inappropriate in the Central American context. Moreover, in the absence of any other institutional arrangements in these countries, one must caution against those U.S. assistance programs that, sometimes purposely and sometimes inadvertently, have helped undermine or discredit existing institutions in Central America before any new ones had been created. While often launched with the best of democratic and developmentalist intentions, some of these programs have had the practical effect of destabilizing Central America still further and of leaving the area with an institutional vacuum.

Left largely to its own devices, approaches, and sometimes crazy-quilt pattern of institutional arrangements, Central America developed rapidly in the 1950s, 1960s, even on into the 1970s. Economic growth was in the range of 5–7 percent per year; social programs were greatly expanded with U.S. assistance; one could even argue that representative institutions were growing—though not necessarily in conformity with U.S.–preferred democratic precepts.[9] Then two main forces, one political and the other economic, converged to undermine this not altogether unattractive picture and to precipitate the crisis in which we now find ourselves.

The political trends involved cloture, sclerosis, and a failure to adjust to new realities. In Nicaragua the authoritarian but not entirely unpopular or unenlightened reign of the father Anastasio Somoza and then his son Luis gave way in the 1970s to the greedy, increasingly corrupt and repressive regime of Anastasio Jr. (Tachito), which finally succeeded in antagonizing all groups in society including the business community and the American embassy. In El Salvador the nationalistic and quasi-progressive combined civil-military system that dominated from 1958 to 1972 was replaced by a brutal and reactionary civil-military faction that sought to turn back the clock, with predictably disastrous consequences. In Guatemala, similarly, the more-or-less centrist regimes that had dominated in the 1960s and early 1970s were replaced by a brutally repressive and corrupt regime that laid the basis for renewed guerrilla resurgence later on. The patterns in these three countries are remarkably similar; they are also the three countries with the largest current difficulties and with which recent U.S. policy has been mainly concerned.[10]

None of these regimes replaced by more brutal, corrupt, and repressive factions had been models of liberalism and democracy by our lights, of course. But they were tolerably efficient, not maintained

125

entirely on the basis of blood and guns, and more-or-less nationalistic and progressive. They were, moreover, able to keep the guerrilla challenges, perpetually present in Central America since the early 1960s, from getting entirely out of hand. Although it is getting ahead of the story, it may be submitted that mixed regimes of this sort are about as much as we can reasonably hope for or expect in Central America.

The second major factor precipitating the current upheaval was economic: the downturn of the Central American economies in the 1970s. Among other factors, the two oil shocks of 1973 and 1979, declining or wildly fluctuating markets for Central American products, and the worldwide economic depression of 1979 and thereafter account for this downturn. The subject has been extensively treated by others, and its details cannot detain us here.[11]

What requires special emphasis, however, is what the economic crisis did to the whole process of Central American change and development. That process, albeit not exclusively democratic, had generally been peaceful and accommodative in the 1950s and 1960s. New groups—the business community, the middle class, some labor groups—had been gradually absorbed into "the system" of Central America in an evolutionary process that was not entirely undemocratic and that resulted in little bloodshed. Accommodative politics is of course relatively easy in a context of an expanding economic pie, since there are always more pieces to hand out to the newer groups without the older and established ones having to be deprived. But in the context of a stagnant or even contracting economic pie, as prevailed in Central America by the late 1970s, there are no new pieces to hand out, and competition for the existing shares tended to become more intense and violent. The response from existing governments was often greater repression.

These indigenous political and economic causes of the Central American crisis were then exacerbated by the intervention of outside forces—principally the Cubans, the Soviets, and eventually the Nicaraguans—into the regional cauldron and by the outsiders' efforts to take advantage of the instability present. Thus, although the Soviets and Cubans are not the prime causes of the rebellion in Central America, it is their presence there that is obviously of most concern to U.S. foreign policy.[12]

It bears reemphasis that the problems in Central America are *systemic problems*.[13] They are long-term, deep rooted, and therefore not amenable to quick or easy solutions. They have evolved from fundamental political, sociological, and economic trends stretching back over twenty years and more. They are not ephemeral or rapidly resolvable. No one single cause provides an adequate explanation for them. Because they are basic, systemic, complex, and long term, they will require long-term, sustained policies and solutions on the part of the United States. I believe it is important for the Commission to stress this to the American people.

At the same time I am not certain the forces at work and the realistic possibilities open are well understood by the American public or, often times, by policy makers. The struggle in Central America is not some dichotomous, either-or struggle between dictatorship and democracy but rather lies generally in those murkier areas of conflict involving combined civilian and military factions jockeying for power and its spoils.[14] How to reach not some ideal and therefore unrealistic solution but one that shows promise of working and a measure of viability given the complex realities of these constant factional struggles, however we might disagree over precise emphases, would seem to me to be a proper concern for U.S. policy. Similarly, we need to differentiate the indigenous from the external causes of the crisis, emphasizing the indigenous causes but showing how and why it is the Cuban and Soviet presences that cause most concern for U.S. policy. The American public and policy makers as well need to be educated as regards both the actualities of Central American domestic politics and sociology and also concerning what is important and not so important to the United States in that part of the world.

Past U.S. Policies

Prior to 1959 Latin America was viewed as a "safe" area for U.S. interests. True, there had been the Guatemalan affair of 1954 but that was considered by policy makers as a temporary aberration that had successfully been reversed. The notion of Stalinist legions expanding into Latin America was, at the time, viewed as preposterous. Hence, with the exception of some limited Point Four and other early assistance programs, Latin America could safely be ignored.[15]

Benign neglect is not an entirely inappropriate policy in easy and peaceful times. In Latin America, however, that stance was maintained too long, obscuring the smoldering problems of the region and therefore catching us unawares and ill-prepared when they eventually exploded. The Cuban Revolution, among other things, meant that Latin America could no longer be ignored.

In response to the Cuban Revolution and also as a reflection of the Kennedy administration's new idealism and dedication to democratic development, the United States launched the Peace Corps and the Alliance for Progress.

A review and evaluation of both these programs would require more space than is possible here. The Alliance requires some attention because its assumptions are often still alive and well in the U.S. government; those same assumptions are current in the present debate over U.S. policy and the proposal for a Central American Marshall Plan. Hence the assumptions of the Alliance and its accomplishments require attention.

The Alliance was posited on the major assumption that economic growth would also produce social and political development that would lead to happy, liberal, pluralist, democratic, middle-class societies just like our own.[16] The goals were not just democratic and developmentalist in an updated Wilsonian sense, however, but also had a major strategic component. That is, they assumed that in such happy and economically modernized societies, middle-class stability would be ensured, extreme ideologies would lose their appeal, the trade unions would embrace collective bargaining rather than radical political action, the military would put aside praetorianism in favor of professionalism and an apolitical stance, business elites would develop a greater sense of noblesse oblige, and so forth.

No one should deny the significant economic accomplishments of the Alliance. Those 5–7 percent growth rates mentioned earlier were in considerable measure due to Alliance pump-priming. The social modernization was also substantial. Anyone visiting Latin America over the last twenty years could not but be struck by the improvements in housing, health care, roads, education, sanitation, water supplies, communications, and a number of other areas—all undertaken with Alliance support.

The political presumptions of the Alliance, however, have not worked out, a fact particularly significant as we consider proposed new campaigns for democratic development. Nowhere in Latin America have happily middle-class societies developed like those of North America or Western Europe—or the hoped-for moderation and stability in politics on which Alliance economic assistance was based. Those countries that are most middle class—Argentina, Chile, Uruguay—could hardly be described as happily, moderately democratic. Nowhere—certainly not in Central America—have extremist ideologies lost their appeal. Nowhere have the trade unions come to accept their proper place in society as docile and apolitical. Nowhere has military professionalization led to an apolitical military; indeed, as Alfred Stepan's work has shown,[17] professionalization of the military may lead to greater, not less, armed forces intervention in politics.

The list of assumptions that have not worked out goes on. Social modernization has led not necessarily to greater stability but often to less, as old institutions are destroyed before viable new ones are created.[18] The country—the Dominican Republic—that received the most per capita aid in the early 1960s and was viewed as a model of the Alliance exploded in left-wing revolution in 1965 calling forth a massive U.S. military intervention that presaged the Vietnam imbroglio. The country—Chile—that received the greatest per capita aid in the late 1960s nevertheless elected a Marxist president in 1970 and then produced one of the most repressive regimes ever seen in Latin America when he was overthrown in 1973.

These comments and examples are not meant to deny the importance of U.S. social and economic assistance to Latin America. Indeed, such assistance is suggested later in this chapter as part of the recommended policy package for Central America. The examples cited do serve, though, to caution against excessive enthusiasm for such aid as a cure-all and against the widespread assumption that such good things as economic development, social modernization, and democracy go inevitably together. Recent development literature strongly implies, in fact, that economic and social modernization may actually be disruptive to political development.[19]

By the late 1960s, corresponding to the height of Vietnam War protests, the early development literature—that of Rostow and others, whose writings had undergirded the Alliance for Progress—was under attack. The Alliance continued to limp along for a time, but with neither the funds nor the enthusiasm of its early, headier days. Samuel P. Huntington and others had weighed in with influential critiques of the development literature, but Huntington's own prescriptions—an emphasis on such agencies as political parties, bureaucracy, and the armed forces, as opposed to social modernization, as the only institutions capable of holding divisive, fragmented third-world countries together—did not seem to work well in Vietnam and came under a considerable cloud. New approaches—for example, meeting basic human needs—were being discussed in the aid agencies, but no consensus had been reached. Indeed, it was precisely this lack of consensus, coupled with growing criticisms of the familiar and existing aid and development approaches, fewer available funds, and preoccupation with Vietnam that diverted attention in policy circles from the rampant problems of Central America.

This new period of not-so-benign neglect produced consequences similar to those that the same strategy had produced in the 1950s. The problems began to accumulate; yet, because of Watergate and other preoccupations, they received little attention. This was precisely the time, however, when the more repressive elements were seizing power and consolidating their hold in El Salvador and Guatemala and when Tachito's greed was going beyond acceptable bounds in Nicaragua. Most scholars and policy analysts look on this period as an opportunity lost in Central America. If we had been more strenuous then in supporting moderate elements, we would not likely face problems of the same magnitude that we face now in the area.

In 1976 Jimmy Carter's emphasis on human rights replaced benign neglect. That strategy, which had earlier echoes in the Kennedy administration and in Woodrow Wilson's naive if well-intentioned efforts to make the world safe for democracy, produced some notable successes. There is no doubt that as a result of the human rights emphasis numerous political prisoners were released from jail, torture was diminished, other abuses were prevented, and the United States received considerable moral credit. Critics, however, charged that the human rights strategy was not even-handed, that it favored some groups and regimes on partisan grounds while ostracizing others, that it was inconsistently applied, that it was inefficiently and heavy-handedly run, that it ignored cultural and societal differences, that it was elevated to such a place that other U.S. interests—economic, strategic— were ignored, and that, in the end, it was not very effective.[20]

While Jimmy Carter emphasized human rights, he no more abandoned American security doctrine than Ronald Reagan abandoned human rights. In fact most analysts, while observing new emphases, have stressed the degree of continuity between the Carter and Reagan administrations.[21] President Carter and his administration began on the left side of the political spectrum and gravitated toward the center; President Reagan began on the right side and grativated toward the center. President Reagan more strongly emphasized the East-West struggle in formulating his Central American policy and considerably increased the U.S. military presence and pressure. Critics charge that a military solution is not likely to solve very much and may produce consequences opposite to those intended. Moreover, they argue, his approach to Central America has done little to resolve the basic, underlying problems that cause revolutionary sentiment to flourish.

The idea is widespread that none of the approaches tried by the United States in Latin America in over thirty years has worked. Certainly the litany of policies outlined here must give pause to those who believe in the ever-onward-and-upwardness theory of U.S. foreign policy directions. These policies have ranged from coexistence with all forms of regimes to blatant military interventionism, from strong activism to benign neglect. It is widely argued in the development field, however, that none of the doctrines of the past really fit Central America,[22] and that U.S. policy, of whatever orientation, has been likewise deficient. Hence the idea for a commission to come up with new approaches.

But many analysts are not convinced that the experiences of the past have been such a dismal failure. While they recognize the flaws in some aspects of policy, they also believe that the overall thrust and record have been not entirely unsound. Mistakes and judgmental errors have certainly occurred in some countries but these analysts point out that, in general and regionwide, notable successes have also been registered. They see the need, hence, not for sweeping new policy designs but for adjustment and updating. They would argue that the basic tenets of a policy oriented toward social, economic, military, and political assistance are not so much flawed in their essentials but that these have been implemented haphazardly and inconsistently by successive administrations. Hence these analysts argue not for some grand as yet untried departures but for a pragmatic eclecticism, choosing and balancing among the proved policies of the past but accommodating to nuance and changed situation and, above all, avoiding the wild fluctuations from administration to administration that they see as the heart of the problem. Let us see what these "new realities" are to which policy must be adjusted.

New Realities in Latin America—and in U.S.–Latin American Relations

Policy, of course, is not formulated in a vacuum. The facts are that Latin America is quite different from what it was two decades back and that the context of U.S.–Latin American relations has changed correspondingly. We have discussed some of these factors before but it is useful to review them here. These new realities need to be factored into any assessment and recommendations for policy. They are presented here in summary form, recognizing that more detailed analysis and qualification are necessary.

1. The United States is now in a generally weaker position vis-à-vis Latin America than was the case fifteen to twenty years ago.[23] Then, U.S. hegemony—military, political, economic, cultural—was overwhelming; today that is no longer the case. Our foreign assistance has lessened, diminishing our leverage; our AID, military, and other missions have been greatly reduced; the American business community is no longer dominant throughout the area; our presence overall is considerably less than it once was; and hence our capacity—or even willingness—to influence events is considerably lessened. We now have fewer levers to manipulate, fewer resources to manipulate them with, and our heart is not really in such dealings. The United States is, of course, *the* dominant power in the region, and our recent buildup

in Central America has partially reversed the earlier trends. This recent involvement, however, is widely viewed as an aberration, unlikely to be sustained over the long haul, a temporary "blip" in a downward-tending graph line. Our heavy present involvement in Central America is viewed as temporary, there is impatience to withdraw, and the assumption is widespread that the trends toward a decreased presence in the area will be resumed shortly once the problem of the moment is resolved.

2. The United States as a political and economic model has been considerably tarnished in recent years. Our economy has not worked so well, our political system shows warts and flaws, our social fabric is perceived to have unraveled somewhat, and our leadership position and stature in the world have been questioned and challenged. Abroad, the American notion that "we know best" for other peoples, in Central America or elsewhere, has been subjected to general skepticism. Latin America no longer wishes so enthusiastically to emulate the United States or necessarily to adopt its political institutions; nor does it wish to follow our foreign policy lead as a matter of course. These changes also imply a more circumspect role for the United States throughout the area.

3. No major new foreign aid program for Central America is likely to be in the offing. Neither the Congress nor the American people are willing to support bold new foreign assistance initiatives.[24] It is unlikely that there could be another Alliance for Progress even if that were desirable; Americans do not want it and we cannot afford it. Indeed, the trends point in the opposite direction: Protectionist walls are being erected, isolationism is rising, and the one major foreign assistance program we have, the Caribbean Basin Initiative, has been so heavily gutted in its crucial trade provisions that one cannot be optimistic about some new, proposed Marshall Plan for the area.

4. There is considerable apprehension, even given the best efforts of this Commission, whether in the present circumstances the United States can carry out a coherent, sustained, bipartisan, long-term foreign policy. The intense and divisive debate over Central American policy, the uncertain fate of the CBI, the irresolution and schizophrenia in American public opinion lend credence to this view. Many seasoned Washington observers—citing the coverage in the popular media of El Salvador and Nicaragua, the strength and independence of some U.S. domestic interest groups who all but carry out their own separate foreign policies, the knotted bureaucratic politics of policy in foreign affairs, the overriding desire for reelection and hence for dramatic headlines on the part of all office holders, the "divided govern-

ment"[25] between president and Congress, and the bitter and partisan nature of the debate—question our very ability to conduct a serious foreign policy. We are so deeply divided that we have reached a stage of near *immobilisme,* and the notion that the main ingredients of a sound policy could be sustained from administration to administration is difficult to credit.[26]

It is arguable whether these constraints on policy are in fact as severe as pictured here, and as to the degree to which they may be or have been reversed. Certainly in Latin America, even in the Caribbean and Central America, despite our most recent preoccupation with the area, the notion of the United States as a floundering, indecisive, and declining superpower is common. These perceptions in the area may be at least as important as any objective assessments to the contrary that we may reach.

5. While the United States would seem to be a diminished or declining presence in Latin America, the Latin American nations themselves have become increasingly assertive and independent. This includes even the smaller nations of Central America, and is especially the case in Mexico. All countries of the area are making various efforts to modify their ties of dependence to the United States, or to redefine or renegotiate the terms of their dependence. This effort at "breaking away" from the United States characterizes right-wing and centrist regimes as well as leftist ones, united in this cause by their rising and intensifying nationalism. A love-hate relationship with the United States has always existed in this region, and that mixed sentiment is by no means confined to one side of the political spectrum. This effort to loosen the bonds with the United States is of course related to Latin America's perception of U.S. power; and to the degree that the Latin American nations perceive the United States as a declining power, prudence requires them to diversify their trade patterns, arms purchases, and international allegiances.[27]

6. At the same time, and to a degree not yet publicly recognized, the United States has become more and more dependent on Latin America, and our interests there have become greater than ever. As our own natural resources have been depleted, we increasingly rely on Latin America for primary goods and raw materials. We need access to the area's markets, and we are increasingly importing both foodstuffs *and* manufactured goods. We are now almost as dependent on Latin America in various ways as it is upon us. Our complex *interdependence* with Latin America is best illustrated by the case of Mexico, where energy policy, immigration policy, trade policy, diplomatic relations, drug traffic, migrant workers policy, and political and

strategic considerations are intertwined in a variety of complex ways.[28]

7. Other outside actors have meanwhile become significant influences in Central America. These include West Germany, France, Japan, Italy, Spain, the Soviet Union, the Scandinavian and Benelux countries, some Eastern European countries, Saudi Arabia, and various transnational agencies (churches, unions, the Socialist International, and foundations). On numerous fronts these other nations and agencies are competing successfully for trade, contracts, business, and political influence. At the same time a number of new regional powers—Cuba, Mexico, Venezuela, Colombia, Argentina, Brazil— have begun to play a more prominent role, one that is generally more independent of the United States. The United States is no longer the only hegemonic power in the hemisphere, and our relations with the area have recently been made much more complex and difficult by the presence of these other actors.[29]

8. Central America itself is changing rapidly. The old beliefs and structures are crumbling, new ones are rising up, the winds of revolution are sweeping the area. *All* the nations are considerably more affluent, developed, self-assured, and independent than they were at the time John F. Kennedy launched the Alliance for Progress. Some have assumed leadership positions in the third world and have put themselves forward as bridges or intermediaries between North and South. Nationalism is powerful, new ideologies have come to the fore not necessarily in accord with the older bases of legitimacy, change and modernization are everywhere in the air. These features, too, affect how the Latin American nations behave and their attitudes toward the United States.[30]

9. Central America is presently going through both a crisis and a period of experimentation. A sense that the U.S. economic and political model may not be appropriate for them is pervasive; yet the Soviet Union has provoked little admiration either. Many Central American thinkers and political leaders are seaching for a new political formula, based on indigenous or national traditions or perhaps combining these with useful and workable imported institutions. The approach will be eclectic; no one set of institutions will be adopted in toto. While this experimentation goes on we can expect considerable instability. Central Americans also plead for some understanding on the part of the United States as they search for that new formula.[31]

10. New issues have come to the fore in inter-American relations. First, economic issues are clearly more important than previously, particularly from a Latin American perspective. While we talk of political and security concerns, their interests lie in economic development. While we speak of the East-West struggle, the Latin Americans,

134

with some prominent exceptions, are more concerned with commercial matters and access to U.S. markets, investments, technology, and capital. While we speak in terms of aid, they talk in terms of trade. This disjuncture in the *agenda* of issues is a major barrier to better relations.

Second, even in terms of more traditional bilateral relations, the issues now are often different. These include such newer but vitally important issues as migration, employment, the drug traffic, human rights, undocumented workers, oil, and the debt situation. These issues are fundamentally distinct from the large political and strategic designs of the 1960s—and they call for a different, more pragmatic U.S. response.[32]

Policy Options

Several policy options have been set forth for Central America, ranging from complete hands-off to a virtual American takeover of the area. While all these options will be duly considered here, it must also be said that they do not all conform equally to the history and new realities of the area, as outlined above. In addition, a number of these options have been tried, with varying degrees of success, in the past. Let us therefore review these options keeping in mind the implications and realistic possibilities of each.

Complete Hands-Off. An influential body of academic opinion suggests that since the United States has so much capacity to do evil in the world and so little to do good, we and the rest of the world would be better off if we did nothing at all. This position goes beyond noninterventionism to suggest a complete hands-off policy, allowing Central America to develop on its own without outside interference.[33]

The troubles with this position are several. First, Central America is as much affected by what we in the United States do not do as by what we do; and cutting ourselves off from trade or contact with Central America would be devastating for that area. Second, although there is an argument for allowing Central America to develop autonomously, it is unlikely that the other outside powers now operating in the region would permit Central America to do so even if the United States were to withdraw. Third, it is inconceivable that the American public or the American government would simply pull up all stakes in Central America and go home. This option is not only undesirable from both a U.S. and a Central American point of view, but also entirely unrealistic.

Benign Neglect, Interspersed with Occasional Involvement. This strategy has been attempted in the past, but it is no longer a useful basis for policy. Although it may have been appropriate in the 1950s when there were no or few perceived threats to U.S. interests in the area, conditions have changed drastically since then. Benign neglect allows problems to fester until they explode rather than providing treatment for them in their early stages. It tends to lead to dramatic intervention (Guatemala in 1954, Cuba in 1961, Chile in 1973) rather than patient resolution of problems over time. Benign neglect also fails to take into account the new reality of our complex *interrelations* with Latin America on a host of issues, meaning that we can no longer ignore the area even if we would choose to do so.[34]

Active Engagement and Democratic Developmentalism. This is probably the most attractive option, especially given the other alternatives. Most scholars and experts on the area, and the general public, would likely support such an option. But there are major problems here as well. These will be discussed below in greater detail. But here let it be said that such active engagement as we practiced in the region in the 1960s may no longer be feasible: The limits on what we can accomplish are greater, the funds and enthusiasm may not be forthcoming, the Central Americans may no longer want such heavy U.S. involvement. In addition, our ability to promote democratic developmentalism, while laudable in theory, runs the danger of being overblown, oversold, exaggerated, unworkable, and therefore productive only of unfulfilled expectations. Some additional cautionary notes follow.

Proconsularism. This approach would have the United States, in effect, take over and run Central America. If the Central Americans cannot resolve their problems, the argument goes, then we should do it for them.

But this approach cannot be effective in the long term. Such a heavy-handed U.S. presence breeds resentment from all sectors in the countries so treated. Moreover, if the long-range goal is the development of indigenous institutions in Central America capable of functioning effectively on their own, then proconsularism will not help create or develop such institutions. It serves in fact to undermine local institutions rather than strengthen them. Except in genuinely emergency situations, proconsularism would leave more problems in its wake that it would immediately resolve.

Gunboat Diplomacy. Except in rare and very special circumstances, the era of gunboat diplomacy in Latin America may well be about over. Such military interventionism unites all Latin Americans against us. Domestically, we seem no longer to have the will for such action, and public opinion is solidly against the commitment of American forces in on-the-ground fighting. Americans tire quickly of indecisive military standoffs, and a policy of military commitment abroad cannot be sustained indefinitely. Gunboat diplomacy tends to respond to the symptoms and not to the causes of upheaval and to leave more problems unresolved than resolved. While it may be an appropriate short-term strategy under exceptional conditions, it is not a basis for long-term policy.

Toward a Prudence Model of U.S. Latin American Policy

Most professional students of Latin America would likely favor option 3 as a long-term basis for U.S. policy: active engagement by the United States in Central America and a policy of democratic developmentalism. Such a policy, however, needs to be reconciled to the new realities already discussed and to the historical and institutional considerations also noted.

First, in the literature it is widely accepted that Central America is going through a profound *systemic* crisis. That crisis is long term and will not be solved quickly or easily. It requires a major and sustained commitment on our part, and to be effective that commitment must necessarily be realistic, consistent, prudent, and bipartisan.

Second, such a policy must be based on the new realities in Latin America, in the United States, and in U.S.–Latin American relations. If these new realities have a sound basis in fact, as most students of the area have concluded, then certain policy prescriptions and guidelines flow from them. It is on the basis of these new realities, I believe, that any recommendations for changes in U.S. foreign policy toward Central America ought to be grounded. What follows therefore represents an effort to reconcile the new hemispheric realities with some broad guidelines for a sound, prudent, and realistic U.S. foreign policy toward the area.[35]

1. The diminished U.S. presence overall throughout the area, the seeming absence of realistic possibilities for some large-scale new design such as the Alliance for Progress, and the corresponding new assertiveness and independence of Latin America all imply some greater prudence and restraint on the part of U.S. policy toward the area. We can no longer work our will there easily, unilaterally, or automatically; the era of deep U.S. involvement in the internal affairs of these countries has not produced the desired results and may be about over. We have neither the inclination nor the means for such

heavy commitments, they seem unlikely to serve the purposes intended, and the expanding presence of other outside actors also implies greater restraint on our part.

The same restraints that now limit unilateral U.S. military action in the hemisphere also impose limits on U.S. political and diplomatic initiatives. A U.S. ambassador, for example, can seldom serve efficaciously any longer in a proconsular capacity as, de facto, the third, second, or maybe *most* important person in the country; nor is it useful to have U.S. mission chiefs running roughshod over local sensibilities by effectively controlling and manipulating those areas of the local national life that come under their purview. Such blatant intervention in the internal affairs of other nations almost always produces unforeseen consequences, leads to profound resentment on the part of all sectors in the country affected, and is certain in the long run to be self-defeating.

There are qualifications to these prescriptions: The formulation above does not take into sufficient account how and when the Congress, public opinion, or legislative requirements such as the certification process may force an American ambassador into a proconsular role; nor does it take account of the degree to which those in the smaller, weaker countries, as distinct from the larger ones, expect us to play a powerful leadership role. Nonetheless, these qualifications do not invalidate the main point: the need over the longer term to forge a policy based on caution, restraint, and balance and to reject heavy-handed interventionism either military or political.

2. U.S. policy must embody a far deeper sense of empathy toward and understanding of these countries than we have heretofore recognized or practiced. The great developmental models and panaceas of the 1960s, mostly of U.S. making, have been discredited or have not worked as intended. The fact is, we do not know best for Central America; and efforts to export our institutions to an area whose culture, mores, and traditions are different from ours have not been notably successful. Central America must be allowed to fashion its own developmental formulas with some timely and appropriate assistance from the United States, not through the replacement of its own institutions with those imposed from the outside. It is prudent and wise for us to desist from exporting our institutions and models to societies where they do not fit, may not be wanted, or may not be deemed appropriate in precisely our form. Not only have such efforts in the past been unsuccessful, but also in the present context we no longer have the resources or commitment to carry out such programs in any case.[36]

A considerably greater degree of empathy and understanding of

Central America on its own terms and in its own institutional framework, however, does not necesssarily imply the acceptance of a Latin American–style Amin or Hitler. We do have values, and we can express them. There are regimes the Latin Americans find unacceptable as well as we. We would do well to follow their lead in these matters. An argument for a greater degree of empathy and cultural relativism in understanding Latin America does not mean we need carry the argument to ridiculous extremes.

3. Likewise with the argument for restraint: Such restraint does not imply we do little or nothing. The key is to find a balanced involvement that falls between benign neglect and heavy-handed interventionism. We have not only values at stake but also increasingly more important interests to protect. The Central American nations, while no longer accepting U.S. hegemony and dominance, do expect us to lead, particularly in the economic field, and to serve as a catalyst, impetus, and locomotive for their own economic recovery.

For example, we should stand for human rights but in a quieter, more restrained, and therefore more effective and less often self-defeating manner than during the Carter administration;[37] we can also be more sensitive to the impact that our statements regarding the priority of human rights concerns have on Latin America, which was not always the case in the early weeks of the Reagan administration. The United States can no longer be the "caudillo of Latin America" with all the strong-arm methods that expression implies, but it can be a prudent bus driver. That metaphor implies that we should drive carefully and well, with due concern for the desired destination of our passengers—neither so slowly that they become impatient and leave the bus, nor so rapidly and far in front that we take the bus in directions the passengers do not wish to go, forcing them to bail out in confusion. Above all, what is called for is consultations with the Central Americans themselves, to ascertain their wants and needs and to adjust U.S. policy accordingly.

4. The key would seem to be active involvement restrained by greater understanding, empathy, prudence than in the past, with an unaccustomed deference to *their* wishes and aspirations. The United States cannot be a mere moral force, which sometimes seemed to be the popular perception of President Carter. That led to a vacuum of hemispheric leadership and produced some unfortunate consequences. Our refusal to sell arms to some regimes deemed morally repulsive, for instance, simply prompted them to buy elsewhere, resulting in an even greater loss of control on our part over their actions and helping precipitate a dangerous arms race throughout the hemisphere whose sour fruits we are now harvesting in the form of escalat-

ing conflict within and between the various Latin American states.

Nor can we elevate the notions of a "global" strategy and "no special relationship" with Latin America to the level of revered truth, which the previous administration also seemed to be doing at times. Those assumptions negate the special relationship that has always existed and still exists in some areas between the United States and Latin America and the requirement of balancing a bilateral and global strategy with a regional one.

But heavy-handed interventionism and cold war rhetoric are not appropriate as a foundation for long-term strategy either. Instead, the United States must act as a catalyst, a fair arbiter, a presence (but not an interventionist one), a leader (but a judicious and temperate one). We are inclined *and* expected to play a leading role in Central America, but that orientation must be tempered by the changing realities described earlier. While accepting and building upon the special relationship that we and the Latin Americans together acknowledge, we must also be cognizant of how this relationship is now changing.

5. Finally, U.S. Latin American policy must be based on realities, not on wishful thinking, myths, and romance. Neither the United States nor Latin America understands the other very well. Our relations are too often governed by moralistic, pietistic, and ideological posturing, often devoid of realism or mutual comprehension. It is time for the relationship to grow up, to achieve a firm and stable basis rather like the United States has with Western Europe, and to eschew condescension and theatrics.

We must not only promote cultural exchanges that flow in both directions but we must also begin to focus on the real issues in hemispheric relations, not phantom ones. In the long run these are not likely (except in a few especially troubled countries) to be the cold war issues that receive so much media attention nor the ambitious political designs of twenty years ago, which now have little support and are, in any case, impractical. Rather, these issues embrace a whole set of new priorities outlined above—above all, trade, markets, and access to capital and technologies. *Our* agenda often focuses on the older political and ideological issues when in fact it is economic issues that form Latin America's chief long-term concern and which, as shown, lie behind the region's political upheavals and are the chief cause of this unrest. Unless we recognize and confront these factors soon, our initiatives and policies and those of Latin America are likely to diverge even further.

Given these general conditions for policy, what more specific recommendations can be suggested? What can we do, and what means are at our disposal? What should U.S. policy be to enhance U.S. interests in the longer term? The proposals that follow remain broad and require even more detailed elaboration, but they do reflect the new realities that we are now facing in the area and coincide with the general guidelines suggested previously that represent an emerging consensus among scholarly experts. These suggestions provide not a single simple answer but encompass a broad matrix of answers that address the complexities of Central America.

Political Strategy. A strategy based on democratic developmentalism but more restrained and less heavy-handed than in the past is required. We must also avoid some of the overdrawn expectations of Project Democracy and of a single-minded campaign to implement these in favor of the more modest goals set forth in the actual legislation. Bloated rhetoric and unrealistic promises should be avoided in formulating this strategy. We will not succeed in transplanting our institutions in Central America or in creating bastions of democracy there, but we may appropriately provide some modest encouragement in the right direction and assist the Central Americans in their own institutional development.

Human Rights Policy. We should favor a strong, visible human rights policy. Nevertheless, that should be balanced against a concern for other preeminent U.S. interests, a sensitivity to foreign cultures whose givens are different from our own, a sensitivity to interventionism in other nations' internal affairs, the requirement of even-handedness, and a subtle and discriminating approach rather than a heavy-handed one.

Military Goals. U.S. military assistance should be continued and maybe even stepped up in some countries, but we should have no illusions that we can create a modern professionalized (by our criteria) military there that will abstain from involvement in civilian politics. That is unrealistic and will not happen, but we should nevertheless continue our training programs and our efforts to get the El Salvadoran military, for example, to see the "bigger picture"—that is that their actions in violating human rights will have a negative impact on congressional votes for aid to El Salvador.[38]

Social Programs. Vastly increased social programs are called for in housing, health care, education, and other areas. Moreover, we need to get our people "on the ground," in the villages the way the Cubans do, so that our assistance is both effective and visible. We need to use our *human* resources far more effectively and to plug into local institutions (neighborhood groups, women's groups, family groups) far more than we do at present. We need to send teachers, doctors, agronomists, and others to operate at grass-roots levels with the empathy and understanding previously called for.

Economic Assistance. A major new economic assistance program is required, which may be called a Marshall Plan for Central America. The program must, of course, recognize the differences between aid to already developed countries temporarily devastated like those in Europe after World War II and aid to noninstitutionalized countries like those in Central America. Appropriate modesty should accompany these proposals so as not to raise exaggerated hopes, either from the point of view of how much aid can be expected from a reluctant public and Congress and how much that aid can accomplish.

The main emphasis, however, should be on trade. That emphasis is most advantageous to us and to the Central Americans. The trade package should include provisions for stable prices for Central America's exports (essential for these single-crop economies), guaranteed access to U.S. markets (enabling them to plan and to be assured of a stable market over a longer term), and access to credit, capital, and technology. These provisions can be carried out in ways that are not detrimental to U.S. industries. Continuous consultations with the nations affected are again required.

Cultural Exchanges. The United States urgently needs to expand its programs of scholarships, training, and travel to the United States for emerging Central American leaders. The Soviet Union and the Eastern European nations are beginning to overwhelm our own efforts in this area. We risk losing an entire generation of young Central American leaders. The provisions of Project Democracy that provide for greater cultural interchange deserve strong support. Some more imaginative new programs are also called for.[39]

Strategic Interests. U.S. security interests should be defined in broad terms that include developmental as well as military assistance. The United States should be prepared to accept a considerable degree of ideological pluralism in Central America, but it should make clear that it will not accept (1) intervention by one state in the internal affairs of another, (2) attacks by one state or another, and (3) an alliance with the Soviet Union that leads to Soviet military bases in the area.[40]

These suggestions are intended as broad guidelines and directions for policy. They provide a framework into which more specific recommendations may be fitted. These more specific suggestions can be appended, or more detailed recommendations can be provided by the particular government agencies—State, AID, etc.—involved. We believed it was important for the Commission to develop a broad conceptual framework first, and that detailed program recommendations could be formulated subsequently.

Conclusion

The intensifying crisis in Central America demonstrates, among other things, that the United States can no longer afford to ignore the area—or to pay attention to it only in crisis times when our capacity to shape the outcome is already severely limited. Our difficulties in coping with the problems of that area also illustrate how limited our knowledge and understanding of Central America are, as well as our tendency to treat it not on its own terms but through the mirror of our own domestic political beliefs and preferences or as an extension of our own election campaigns. Neither moral prejudgments, wishful thinking, nor exaggerated rhetorical flourishes are sufficient to achieve the measured, balanced policy that is required, or to enable us to deal responsibly with the dynamics of sociopolitical change in the area in the context of its own practices and institutions rather than through our own rose-colored lenses.

The reorientation of policy suggested here—toward greater prudence, some modesty, greater empathy, and restraint in our attitudes and actions toward the area, coupled with the more specific policy prescriptions that followed—would seem to be both practical and wise. The United States, because of its own preference and power and because of the expectations of the Central Americans themselves, can be a leader—and not just a moral leader—in the area; but such power and leadership also imply restraint and forbearance. While the United States can serve as a bastion of freedom and human rights, policies in these areas need to be practical, kept in perspective, and attuned to the distinct nuances such key terms convey to the two parts of the Americas.

We can and must adjust to the new realities of Latin America without presuming either to lead the change process ourselves or to stand irrevocably and hostilely against Latin America's own, quite natural processes of change. We can, as well, continue to maintain a strong military in addition to a strong political and economic influence in the area, while also exercising moderation in the use of such influence. We may even be able to use some tough rhetoric and action sometimes for a domestic political audience, as long as it is made clear to the nations of the area that other kinds of discussions and negotiations can go on in private. There are, moreover, ways to balance domestic economic concerns while also making provision for Latin American access to our markets—access that the Central American countries desperately require, without which the political conflicts of the area are bound to worsen, and hence that comes first on Latin America's agenda if not yet on our own.

Such a strategy of greater prudence, empathy, and restraint is not only best for us in the long term, but it is also, most important, firmly grounded in the new realities of Latin America and our relations with it. It responds to the somewhat diminished presence and influence of the United States in that part of the world in a way that enables us to continue to play a strong and positive role. It allows and encourages us to act as a catalyst and "locomotive" while also taking cognizance of the circumscribed limits on what the United States can and cannot effectively do in that area. It reflects the growth and influence of other outside powers besides ourselves in the area and enables us to adjust realistically to the complexities of policy that the presence of these other actors necessitates. It reflects also the growing assertiveness and independence of the Latin American nations, their desire to diversify their trade and international connections, and the need for us realistically to adjust to these newer currents. Finally, such a strategy enables us to continue to play a leadership role in the region, in both the politico-strategic and the economic spheres, in ways that both we and the Central Americans desire—but to do so with considerably greater wisdom, empathy, and enlightenment than in the past.

Notes

1. The better books include Thomas P. Anderson, *Politics in Central America* (New York: Praeger, 1982); H. Michael Erisman and John D. Martz, eds., *Colossus Challenged: The Struggle for Caribbean Influence* (Boulder, Colo.: Westview Press, 1982); Richard Feinberg, ed., *Central America: International Dimension of the Crisis* (New York: Holmes and Meier, 1982); Richard Millett and Marvin Will, eds., *The Restless Caribbean* (New York: Praeger, 1979); and Howard J. Wiarda, ed., *Rift and Revolution: The Central American Imbroglio* (Washington, D.C.: American Enterprise Institute, 1984).

2. A parallel paper, focused on the Caribbean Basin rather than on Central America, and stressing more the background of the area than policy prescriptions, is Howard J. Wiarda, "Changing Realities and U.S. Policy in the Caribbean Basin: An Overview," in *Western Interests and U.S. Policy Options in the Caribbean Basin* (Washington, D.C.: Atlantic Council, 1984); chapter 6 in this volume.

3. At a session of the Atlantic Council's Working Group on Western Inter-

ests and U.S. Policy Options in the Caribbean Basin, Washington, D.C., Spring 1983.

4. On Project Democracy see Howard J. Wiarda, "Can Democracy Be Exported? The Quest for Democracy in United States Latin American Policy," Paper prepared for the Inter-American Dialogue on U.S.–Latin American Relations in the 1980s, The Latin America Program of the Woodrow Wilson International Center for Scholars, Washington, D.C., March 1983, forthcoming in a volume edited by Kevin Middlebrook and Carlos Rico.

5. Edward Banfield, *The Moral Basis of a Backward Society* (New York: Free Press, 1958).

6. Samuel P. Huntington, *Political Order in Changing Societies* (New Haven, Conn.: Yale University Press, 1968).

7. Murdo J. Macleod, *Spanish Central America: A Socioeconomic History* (Berkeley: University of California Press, 1973).

8. Thomas L. Karnes, *The Failure of Union: Central America 1824–1975* (Tempe: Arizona State University, Center for Latin American Studies, 1976).

9. For overviews of each country see Howard J. Wiarda and Harvey F. Kline, *Latin American Politics and Development* (Boston, Mass.: Houghton-Mifflin, 1979).

10. More detailed analysis is contained in Anderson, *Politics in Central America*.

11. Feinberg, *Central America*; and Gary Wynia, "Setting the Stage for Rebellion: Economics and Politics in Central America's Past," in Wiarda, *Rift and Revolution*.

12. See especially Jiri and Virginia Valenta, "Soviet Strategy and Policies in the Caribbean Basin," in Wiarda, *Rift and Revolution*.

13. This is one of the principal conclusions of the Atlantic Council's study project on "Western Interests and U.S. Policy Options in the Caribbean Basin"; see the final policy paper prepared by Richard Feinberg with Robert Kennedy.

14. See Howard J. Wiarda, ed., *The Continuing Struggle for Democracy in Latin America* (Boulder, Colo.: Westview Press, 1980).

15. The best study is Robert A. Packenham, *Liberal America and the Third World: Political Development Ideas in Foreign Aid and Social Science* (Princeton, N.J.: Princeton University Press, 1973).

16. Max F. Millikan and W. W. Rostow, *A Proposal: Key to an Effective Foreign Policy* (New York: Harper, 1957); also Rostow, *The Stages of Economic Growth: A Non-Communist Manifesto* (Cambridge: Cambridge University Press, 1960).

17. Alfred Stepan, *The Military in Politics: Changing Patterns in Brazil* (Princeton, N.J.: Princeton University Press, 1971).

18. That was a major finding by Huntington in *Political Order in Changing Societies*.

19. Packenham, in *Liberal America*, makes these arguments in great detail.

20. Larman C. Wilson, "Human Rights in United States Foreign Policy: The Rhetoric and the Practice," in Donald C. Piper and Ronald C. Terchek, eds., *Interaction: Foreign Policy and Public Policy* (Washington, D.C.: American Enterprise Institute, 1983), pp. 178–208.

21. Paul Sigmund, "Latin America: Change or Continuity?" *Foreign Affairs*, vol. 60 (1981), pp. 629–57; Susan Kaufman Purcell, "Carter, Reagan et l'Amerique Centrale," *Politique Etrangère*, vol. 47 (June 1982), pp. 309–17; Abraham F. Lowenthal, "Ronald Reagan and Latin America: Coping with Hegemony in Decline," in Kenneth Oye et al., *Eagle Defiant: United States Foreign Policy in the 1980s* (Boston: Little, Brown, 1983), pp. 311–35; and Howard J. Wiarda, "The United States and Latin America: Change and Continuity," in Alan Adelman and Reid Reading, eds., *Stability/Instability in the Caribbean* (Pittsburgh, Pa.: University of Pittsburgh Press, forthcoming); chapter 3 in this volume.

22. Packenham, *Liberal America*; also Howard J. Wiarda, *Politics and Social Change in Latin America: The Distinct Tradition*, 2d rev. ed. (Amherst: University of Massachusetts Press, 1982).

23. On this see especially Abraham F. Lowenthal, "The United States and Latin America: Ending the Hegemonic Presumption," *Foreign Affairs*, vol. 55 (October 1976), pp. 199–213.

24. John E. Reilly, "The American Mood: A Foreign Policy of Self-Interest," *Foreign Policy*, vol. 34 (Spring 1979), pp. 74–86.

25. Glen Gordon, *The Legislative Process and Divided Government* (Amherst: University of Massachusetts, Bureau of Government Research, 1966).

26. These trends are discussed at greater length in the earlier chapters of this book.

27. Discussed at greater length in chapter 6.

28. See the contributions by Fred Bergsten, David Macdonald, Otto Reich, and H. Jon Rosenbaum in Howard J. Wiarda and Janine T. Perfit, eds., *Trade, Aid, and U.S. Economic Policy in Latin America* (Washington, D.C.: American Enterprise Institute, 1983).

29. Feinberg, *Central America*.

30. As discussed and documented in Wiarda, *Politics and Social Change* and *Latin American Politics and Development*.

31. *Ibid*; also Howard J. Wiarda, "Toward a Non-Ethnocentric Theory of Development: Alternative Conceptions from the Third World," *Journal of Developing Areas* (July 1983).

32. See the author's contribution to the Atlantic Council study cited above, "Changing Realities and U.S. Policy in the Caribbean Basin"; chapter 6 in this book.

33. In some circles this option is known as the "Cambodian model"; it is not looked on as advantageous by the more pragmatic Central American leaders, even those thought of as on the left.

34. Packenham, in *Liberal America*, discussed this and other options at length.

35. An earlier version of these proposals was presented in "Conceptual and Political Dimensions of the Crisis in U.S.–Latin American Relations," Paper written for the AEI Public Policy Week Forum of December 7, 1982; published in Howard J. Wiarda, ed., *The Crisis in Latin America* (Washington, D.C.: American Enterprise Institute, 1984).

36. These arguments are presented at greater length in Wiarda, "Can De-

mocracy Be Exported?"; some more positive suggestions are contained in the author's "Project Democracy in Latin America: Reservations and Suggestions," Paper prepared for a conference on Project Democracy, United States Information Agency, Washington, D.C., May 9, 1983.

37. Howard J. Wiarda, "Democracy and Human Rights in Latin America: Toward a New Conceptualization," *Orbis*, vol. 22 (Spring 1978), pp. 137–60; also Wiarda, ed., *Human Rights and U.S. Human Rights Policy* (Washington, D.C.: American Enterprise Institute, 1982).

38. See the report of Curtis S. Morris, Jr., "The United States–Caribbean Basin Military Connection: A Perspective on Regional Military-to-Military Relationships," (Center for Hemispheric Studies, American Enterprise Institute, Occasional Paper, no. 7, Washington, D.C., 1983).

39. For some suggestions see Wiarda, "Project Democracy."

40. These suggestions follow those contained in the Atlantic Council "Policy Paper"; that report contains many other policy recommendations worthy of study by the Commission.

SELECTED AEI PUBLICATIONS

AEI Foreign Policy and Defense Review (six issues $18; single copy, $3.50)

The Crisis in Latin America: Strategic, Economic, and Political Dimensions, Howard J. Wiarda, ed., with Mark Falcoff and Joseph Grunwald (32 pp., $2.95)

Rift and Revolution: The Central American Imbroglio, Howard J. Wiarda, ed. (392 pp., cloth $19.95, paper $10.95)

Interaction: Foreign Policy and Public Policy, Don C. Piper and Ronald J. Terchek, eds. (235 pp., cloth $16.95, paper $8.95)

Terrorism: What Should Be Our Response? John Charles Daly, mod. (25 pp., $3.75)

A Conversation with Dr. Saddoun Hammadi: Iraq's Foreign Policy (14 pp., $2.25)

Conversations with Harold H. Saunders: U.S. Policy for the Middle East in the 1980s (101 pp., $5.25)

Human Rights and U.S. Human Rights Policy, Howard J. Wiarda (96 pp., $4.25)

Prospects for a New Lebanon, Elie Salem (14 pp., $3.75)

• *Mail orders for publications to:* AMERICAN ENTERPRISE INSTITUTE, 1150 Seventeenth Street, N.W., Washington, D.C. 20036 • *For postage and handling, add 10 percent of total; minimum charge $2, maximum $10* • *For information on orders, or to expedite service, call toll free 800-424-2873* • *When ordering by International Standard Book Number, please use the AEI prefix—0-8447* • *Prices subject to change without notice* • *Payable in U.S. currency only*

AEI ASSOCIATES PROGRAM

The American Enterprise Institute invites your participation in the competition of ideas through its AEI Associates Program. This program has two objectives: (1) to extend public familiarity with contemporary issues; and (2) to increase research on these issues and disseminate the results to policy makers, the academic community, journalists, and others who help shape public attitudes. The areas studied by AEI include Economic Policy, Education Policy, Energy Policy, Fiscal Policy, Government Regulation, Health Policy, International Programs, Legal Policy, National Defense Studies, Political and Social Processes, and Religion, Philosophy, and Public Policy. For the $39 annual fee, Associates receive

- a subscription to *Memorandum,* the newsletter on all AEI activities
- the AEI publications catalog and all supplements
- a 30 percent discount on all AEI books
- a 40 percent discount for certain seminars on key issues
- subscriptions to two of the following publications: *Public Opinion,* a bimonthly magazine exploring trends and implications of public opinion on social and public policy questions; *Regulation,* a bimonthly journal examining all aspects of government regulation of society; and *AEI Economist,* a monthly newsletter analyzing current economic issues and evaluating future trends (or for all three publications, send an additional $12).

Call 202/862-6446 or write: AMERICAN ENTERPRISE INSTITUTE
1150 Seventeenth Street, N.W., Suite 301, Washington, D.C. 20036